Why Service Stinks

...and Exactly What to Do About It!

T. Scott Gross

Dearborn™
Trade Publishing
A **Kaplan Professional** Company

Vice President and Publisher: Cynthia A. Zigmund
Acquisitions Editor: Jonathan Malysiak
Senior Managing Editor: Jack Kiburz
Interior Design: Lucy Jenkins
Cover Design: Scott Rattray, Rattray Designs
Typesetting: Elizabeth Pitts

Published by Dearborn Trade Publishing
A Kaplan Professional Company

Library of Congress Cataloging-in-Publication Data

Gross, T. Scott.
    Why service stinks—and exactly what to do about it! / by T. Scott
Gross.
        p. cm.
        ISBN 0-7931-7681-6 (6 × 9 paperback)
    1. Customer services. I. Title.
    HF5415.5.W763 2003
    658.8′12—dc22

                                              2003016503

Dearborn Trade books are available at special quantity discounts to use for sales promotions, employee premiums, or educational purposes. Please call our Special Sales Department to order or for more information at 800-245-2665, e-mail trade@dearborn.com, or write to Dearborn Trade Publishing, 30 South Wacker Drive, Suite 2500, Chicago, IL 60606-7481.

DEDICATION

You'll get to know her as you read the book, but for now let me tell you that Melanie Gross, aka Buns, is one of the smartest, sweetest folks on the entire planet. She is my hero. She is also my best friend, lover, confidante, and forever partner. And I could not, would not, be me without her.

OTHER BOOKS BY T. SCOTT GROSS

Contents

PART FOUR

IT'S ALL ABOUT THE CUSTOMER

When I launched myself in the wee hours of the morning from the warm spot next to Buns to peck the last bit of inspiration into my computer, I had been thrashing the sheets for what seemed like an eternity, rolling the final bit of thinking for this book around in my mind like a pinball going everywhere. I thought about waiting until the morning, or at least a more agreeable part of the morning, to make my notes.

I was certain I would remember the new ideas for gathering the research; I would remember the analogy of rock-paper-scissors (which turned out not to be a big idea). But there, daring me to get up, was the memory of an old Earl Nightingale tape in which he makes the point that what separates the winners from the losers is that winners are willing to do things that losers will not, such as get out of bed in the middle of the night rather than risk losing a good idea or two.

And that's precisely what this book is about—the differences that make us unique and influence whether I am going to give you awful service, indifferent service, pretty good service, or all the way to Positively Outrageous Service.

I have been a student of customer service for many years. Now, finally, I am going to look into the minds of the folks that served you dinner last night or took your payment at the airport parking lot and answer the question, "What were they thinking?"

By the way, we might as well look at what *you* are thinking.

There are three types of folks who are going to read this book. First are the service pros who bought the book on their own simply because they love customers and are always looking for ways to serve them better. Read on, and you'll learn why the things you've been doing intuitively work. Then you will be able to do them with a sense of understanding and purpose. If you are a service pro, you won't be disappointed.

The second type is the vast middle ground, folks who already treat customers nicely but aren't prone to falling in love every time one walks through the door. For you I've made the book easy to read and have packed in as many ideas as possible for making it easy to love customers even if it doesn't feel natural.

Finally are the folks who woke with a start the instant the boss dropped this book on their desk and said, "You'd better read this. T. Scott Gross is speaking at our conference, and he wants you to take some kind of test."

Hey, don't blame me, he's *your* boss! For you, we've made this easier than easy. Just skim through the book and read the stuff in the little boxes. It's like having a book with built-in Cliffs Notes.

Ask any American about the state of customer service, and nearly all will tell you that it is miserable and trending to worse. Fine, but if everyone says service is awful and all servers will tell you that they personally deliver great service, who is it that is giving all that poor service?

Why Service Stinks . . . and Exactly What to Do about It is based on serious research that gets to the bottom of poor service as well as explores the origins of good service. I chose as my research partner ACCORD Management Systems of Westlake Village, California, the leading experts in employee selection and succession and the decisions that create win-win promotions.

Also on the team are the good folks at BIGresearch, *the* source for online market research. And, of course, there are the thousands of very vocal consumers who took the time to tell us what they were thinking.

I wanted to discover how the attitudes of the manager, the server, and the customer interact to determine exactly what service is actually delivered. I wondered if I could predict the service outcome of any combination of boss-server-customer behavior.

We (my research team and I) have interviewed servers and clerks, whether they are known for delivering great customer service or likely to totally offend valuable clients. And I haven't forgotten the rest of the equation: bosses and customers who, as you'll see, have a lot more influence over the quality of service than you or they might imagine.

I've done my homework, and now you are about to discover the answer to that age-old quandary of why service stinks!

This book is current as of October 4 at 3:11 AM. Well, not exactly. It's really current as of . . . right now! Nope, I missed it again. Well, here's the deal. This book will always be current so long as you can access <www.tscottgross.com>, where the research is ongoing, a constant stream of Internet input. You can add your thoughts to the mix and, in at least a minor way, influence the way people think about customer service and leadership.

I'll talk more about the research and the wonderful folks who have participated so far, but for now why don't you read on? I'll get dressed!

A *c k n o w l e d g m e n t s*

It would be wrong of me not to mention Stuart, my younger, better-looking brother, whose job it is to keep me on the road so that the bills (and he) get paid! I didn't say that he actually helped with the book, only that it would be wrong not to mention him. So, hi, Stu!

Thanks to Rocketta Springman, who was a huge help with the research as well as with keeping up with her already busy schedule running our office, and to Shannon Bernes of ACCORD Management Systems, whose assistance was invaluable.

If you can thank someone anonymously, we'll do it here and say thanks to the dozens of companies that answered questions and participated by allowing us to profile their service teams.

Finally, yo, Buns! Thanks for being my editor even when you cringe at the words you claim I invented!

IT'S ALL ABOUT THE TEAM

1

WHAT WERE THEY THINKING?

Customer service is a product. It's one of the few products—maybe the only one—that is produced one at a time, on the spot, and customized by definition for each individual customer. And what's really scary is it can't be returned for credit.

Or maybe even scarier, when it comes to delivering the customer service product, it is rarely practical for the boss to supervise each and every delivery! "Your call may be monitored for quality control and training purposes." Nonsense! You can't watch everyone all the time. And mystery shoppers? I recommend them, but they won't catch everything.

The biggest customer service joke is the idea of empowerment. The concept is fine, but the execution, miserable.

Corporations of all sizes have been jumping onto the empowerment bandwagon as though they can actually confer empowerment as if it were tangible. They can't. Every cop with a gun is empowered to shoot. Every paramedic with a laryngoscope is empowered to intubate. And every employee, no matter his or her job status, has the power, if not the authority, to totally tick off your best customer.

And you can't stop it.

I've been thinking that there may be a way to prevent bad service by bringing together the elements that add to good, even great, service.

I actually have an answer to that question so often asked with pure astonishment: How can service people be so stupid or uncaring? I'm about to tell you what it is they were thinking!

TO READ OR NOT TO READ, THAT IS THE QUESTION!

The flight was nearly four hours, and the small plane seemed to grow smaller by the moment. I had two thoughts. Landing this thing was the first thought, but the one that carried me to the runway involved a glass of iced tea the size of a house. It was nearly 100 muggy degrees on the tarmac, which made the last few steps to the general aviation terminal feel as though Dante should be waiting at the door.

She sat just inside the door, not Dante but close enough. She was reading a novel from her perch behind the counter. I didn't care. She wasn't exactly on my payroll, and it was the thought of iced tea that propelled me to the pilots lounge.

I turned the corner and reached the spot where I knew there would be a large metal urn sweating on the outside and brimful of refreshment on the inside. But the urn was empty, turned upside down, drier than parchment.

"Hey!" I didn't exactly shout, but I wanted to be heard all the way to the reception desk. "There's no iced tea!"

I peeked back around the corner and noticed that the novel never budged.

"I know." She sounded incredulous as if she too had difficulty imagining that service had gone straight to hell. "The lineman was so busy this morning he didn't have time to make tea or do much of anything except fuel planes."

By now I had reversed course and was headed out. Any destination with a plentiful supply of iced tea was going to work for me.

"Well, maybe somebody else could learn how to make tea." The door banged shut and I can't say if there was a reply.

What I *can* say is this: If you were to ask the receptionist what kind of service she delivers, she would be amazed that you would even bother to ask.

"Why, I give great service! All my customers love me!"

What was she thinking?

BONUS WORDS—EXTRA BISCUITS

Sometimes simply asking "What were they thinking?" is much too kind for the situation. For this next one, even Jay Leno couldn't resist spreading the tale.

A fried chicken restaurant employee was working the drive-through as a second job. No, it would be more accurate to say that he was working the drive-through *and* a second job, both at the same time.

He was selling pot. From the drive-through! Does that strike you as stupid? Well, don't be so judgmental! This rocket scientist had a plan. Only those folks who knew the secret password would receive the illegal goodies.

The password?

"I'd like extra biscuits, please."

Who would have guessed? What were they thinking?

Dumbing Down the Job

For what seemed like the longest time, my wife and I owned a fast-food fried chicken restaurant. It would be fair to say it was fun, but it was also frustrating. Owning the restaurant was like going to the lab every morning and running an experiment to discover what our employees were thinking. Sometimes it appeared they weren't thinking at all.

There was the time I was working the drive-through, one of my favorite things to do because things move so fast that once you get in your groove serving hot, fried chicken, the effort takes on an almost balletlike quality. (I may have overstated the point; sorry!)

During one particularly hot and heavy dinner rush, I was backed up by a 16-year-old employee working one of his first few shifts. So I didn't expect a lot, but I was surprised when he said, "How do you do that?"

"Do what?" I never stopped moving. The sweat was dripping off the end of my nose.

"Do that." He pointed to the register that I was playing like a piano and taking a shortcut that got the drawer open faster than usual. The usual way was to enter the amount tendered and let the register calculate the change.

"Oh, well, instead of entering the amount tendered and then hitting enter, I just hit enter and the drawer opens. It's faster."

"No, how do you know how much change to give them?"

"It's a secret," I confided without breaking my rhythm. "Only old people know how to do that!"

Have we dumbed down jobs to the point that when employees are finally called on to make a decision, they either cannot or will not?

Sometimes it's not so much that your employees are thinking stupidly. They may not know how to think at all. That sounds worse than I intended. They may only need training. On the other hand . . .

We're Not Kmart Capital One

It was 9:30, and the phone was ringing, but it was unlikely to be anyone we knew. (Friends of old people know to call early.) Besides, we're always getting calls for Kmart Capital One on our 800 number.

"Hello, this is Scott."

"I need to check my balance."

"I'm sorry, you have the wrong number."

"How do you know?" (This guy works somewhere.)

You Won't Believe . . .

Buns and I stopped for a taco and a giant iced tea. It was a national franchise place, so I expected it to be clean, the tacos to be so-so, and the service . . . well, you take your chances.

The guy in front of us ordered more tacos than I could eat in a lifetime. The total was $19.10. Trying to be helpful, he handed the server a twenty-dollar bill and a dime.

Pencils *down*!

Somehow the server managed to get the amount tendered entered as an imaginary number, and the cash drawer refused to budge. I tried to communicate via mental telepathy, which sometimes works but only if there is a receiver. "Open the drawer," I willed. "Give him a dollar." She was frozen.

I was considering giving the guy a dollar myself just to get the line moving when the assistant manager materialized, saying, "Let me handle this, Evelyn. I've been to training school."

I knew he would take out his register key, give the guy a buck, and then smile triumphantly at the next customer in line and say, "May I hep yeeuuw?" (Remember this happened in Texas!)

But he didn't. He took out his pocket calculator . . .

What was that boy thinking?

Muffins Aren't for Breakfast Anymore

Once in a while a good raisin bran muffin sounds good to me, but I live in the boonies, where the muffins aren't that easy to find. One Sunday morning, in a fit of uncontrolled optimism, I launched myself to the nearest supermarket and began to prowl for a muffin. No muffins.

"Excuse me. I can't find any raisin bran muffins."

"We don't have none."

"You don't have any?" I corrected gently, more for my benefit than hers.

"Right, we don't have none. I recognize you. You always come in here looking for raisin bran muffins, and we never have any. You can come back after while."

"After while as in 30 minutes? After while as in later today? Or after while as in October?"

"It's too early. We don't have none until after lunch."

I asked for the department manager.

"Hi, I'm Scott and I usually come in . . . "

"I know . . . looking for a raisin bran muffin. We don't bake the muffins until after lunch. You should buy muffins after lunch while we still have some."

"But muffins are sort of a breakfast thing, and if you are worried about running out, *you're out right now!*"

That last part I didn't shout. Actually, I didn't say it at all. I just let the thought die before it reached my lips and instead left the store wondering, "What were they thinking?"

Sale? What Sale?

Linda of Burlington, Vermont, wrote: "I entered an upscale shoe store that resides on the same pedestrian mall as my own store. Since I own an art material store, dressing nicely is only an invitation to explode a tube of paint on you, hence, my 'uniform' of jeans and a sweater.

"After receiving the usual deadly greeting of 'Can I help you?' I explained that I was looking for a nice pair of loafers. The sales associate's reply was 'You'll probably want to shop on the clearance racks, right?'

"Wrong. Goodbye. Haven't been in since. Will never go in again."

Hurry Up and Wait

The week had been incredible—six speaking engagements in seven days on a run that stretched from Palm Springs to Puerto Rico. Buns and I were on the final leg with a change of planes at JFK and then on to Logan. The night was cool, overcast, and drizzling. The long, over-the-water approach to runway four-left had me nervous as a cat. But the landing was fine, the taxiing forever, and the layover a mere 45 minutes. (Scheduled, that is.)

After a long hustle to the commuter gates, our spirits sagged to see the 8:05 departure moved to 8:40. No problem. My newest thing is patience, and here would be a perfect chance to get in some practice.

The schedule changed again. Now we're talking 9:20, which stretched yet again to 10:00 PM. Some time after 10, a PA announcement informed us that the crew was running late and boarding would be soon. About an hour after my patience practice was called off, we were herded onto a shuttle for the short ride to the commuter plane.

I could have driven to Boston and been in bed.

Into the rain and onto the shuttle, the good news was that we were finally about to get under way. So we stood near the door sucking in diesel fumes and waiting for the driver.

Ten minutes, then 15. At 20 the crowd grew restless. Twenty-five, now 30 minutes. Do I hear 36? Thirty-six minutes standing on a bus waiting for a flight that takes . . . 36 minutes? Hello?

A gate agent stepped aboard and said, "We're waiting for a connecting passenger. Sorry about the wait."

Quick quiz: Do you think the gate agents were . . .

1. stupid?
2. mean-spirited?
3. unconscious?
4. all of the above?

Quick quiz, part two: The gate agents, when asked about the state of customer service, are likely to say . . .

1. We give great service but service elsewhere is the pits.
2. We are part of the problem, definitely.
3. Our service would be better if we had better bosses.
4. Customers should know better than to fly on rainy nights.

Cold under the Collar

We met our friends, lovingly nicknamed Pitstop and Repo, for a quick lunch at a Mexican restaurant that was new to us and a favorite of theirs. It was the first crisp day of fall, the kind of day when you hurry to and from the car rather than wear a jacket and then wonder why you were so lazy.

Once inside we discovered that fall had also arrived at the restaurant. The AC was cranked all the way to frosty. Brrr!

"Somewhere toasty," I asked the greeter in the tight white shorts.

Naturally, she selected a four-top immediately below a ceiling fan that was churning at high revs.

I'm tall. No problem. I pulled the chain. Ahhh, better!

The server arrived, took our order, and reached for the chain.

"Excuse me! Can we leave that off until we defrost, please?"

There was no hesitation, just a quick explanation followed by an even quicker tug on the chain!

"We like to leave the fans on. It makes it cooler in the kitchen." Mr. Awareness turned and walked away quickly.

Had he stayed I would have said . . . "I probably should tell you that usually I take medication that helps keep me from being violent. And I skipped my pill today."

Or my all-time favorite, "It's okay by me. It's your tip!"

Instead, I just stood in place, reached for the chain, and the world was good again. But I was left wondering, "What were they thinking?"

THE SOLUTION

If there was a solution, a single, one-size-fits-all solution, it would be this: Think like a customer. And that would lead us to the Golden Rule, which all by itself is a pretty good rule.

Unfortunately, that won't work. Because if you personally were thinking like a customer and following the Golden Rule, service at your place could still be the pits. Think about the times you have received awful service and thought to yourself, "I'd bet if the owner knew what was happening in her store today, she'd have a fit." Probably so.

The answer is simple but not easy: Hire Service Naturals.

Why? Because thinking like customers and following the Golden Rule comes naturally to Service Naturals. There's no training, no policies, and no batteries required.

2

WHEN CUSTOMERS TALK

What we know is this: Although there is a best service personality for any given service situation, *no single personality profile is best for every service situation.* The chief variables are boss, customer, and environment. And the biggest variable of the three, I believe, is the customer. How else can you explain that where one customer has fallen in love, another is turned away in disgust?

I decided to go right to the source by asking 10,000 customers what they think about the state of service in the United States. My research team and I also asked them who they think is to blame and what strategies they use for getting what they want.

Here is a great place to thank the good folks at BIGresearch.com for handling the survey work! BIGresearch is the nation's premier consumer market intelligence firm and monitors the pulse of over 8,000 consumers monthly. BIGresearch is the consumer intelligence voice of the National Retail Federation and the Retail Advertising and Marketing Association.

When you write a book titled *Why Service Stinks* and offer to explain, it begs the question, "Says who?" It's funny that you should ask! It turns out that not everyone says that service stinks. I, for one, think that customer service is actually pretty good. And I'm not alone. A minority of those surveyed (2.3 percent) rated customer service in America as excellent, and a surprising 28 percent rated customer service as good. That's nearly one out of three of us who think that customer service doesn't stink at all!

Nearly half (45.7 percent) say that customer service is merely average, but average and stinking aren't quite in the same ballpark. Actually, only a picky 3.8 percent would say that service actually stinks.

The weighted average response on a scale of 1 to 5, with 5 being excellent and 1 being el stinko rio, was a slightly above average 3.05 percent. I guess you could call that good news, but some of us don't want to be average. Some of us think great customer service is a significant business advantage, and average just doesn't cut it.

So we asked our panel to tell us *why* service is not always good. Here's what they said, listed in order of importance from most important to least important:

1. Servers who just don't care (The wrong person in the wrong position)
2. Servers who aren't properly trained (It's not their fault!)
3. Bosses who fail to schedule sufficient help (Not the servers' fault!)
4. Customers who are rude (It's your fault!)
5. Customers who are impatient (Your fault, again!)

I'd be hard-pressed to blame servers for any of the above reasons for poor service, including servers who just don't care. After all, they are likely to be highly stressed working in a job that is not compatible with their personality!

Most customers are pretty savvy when it comes to negotiating their way through their daily purchases. We think this is because customers are servers too! Most customers know what it's like to be on the other side of the counter, and most have developed strategies for getting their way.

Mine is humor. I've been known to wade into a clutch of B-S-ing salesclerks saying, "Alright! Who called this meeting and why wasn't I invited?" That usually breaks the ice, but few normal people would be comfortable with that.

Nope, the tactic our survey said was most likely to get good customer service is simply *asking for exactly what you want.*

Just yesterday we trooped into the Old Spanish Trail Café for a burrito fix. I asked for iced tea the size of a house and a Burrito Supreme drowned in chili, smothered in cheese, and covered completely with jalapenos. And that is exactly what I got! (Rolaids are not included!)

And it helps to be a regular. As we walked into the restaurant, I overheard one of the waitresses say, "The burrito guy is here."

What techniques work? Well, as Richard Dawson would have said, "Survey says . . . " (listed in order of effectiveness):

- *Ask for exactly what you want.* (This is the number one tactic. Try it!)
- *Be a frequent customer.* (Be known. They know you will be back!)
- *Use humor to engage the server.* (This is a matter of establishing a connection.)
- *Tip big.* (This is not at the top of the list because it's after the fact!)
- *Dress well.* (Does this mean you must be a person of substance?)
- *Call the server by name.* (Deny anonymity.)

And what doesn't work? (Welcome to the 21st century!)

- *Ask to talk to the boss.* (This is *not* helpful.)
- *Deal with someone who is the same race as yourself.* (Race doesn't matter.)
- *Deal with someone who is the same sex as yourself.* (This ranks right up there with calling the server "Honey!")

While we had their attention, we decided to ask how customer service impacted their shopping habits. We asked:

How far out of your way are you willing to drive for better service?

Less than a mile	7.2%
2–3 miles	12.0
4–5 miles	19.0
6–10 miles	25.4
11–15 miles	10.3
16–20 miles	9.2
More than 20 miles	16.9

As you can see from the above numbers, great customer service can easily erase the handicap of a poor location!

When I get really bad service, I am likely to tell others.

Yes	96.1%
No	3.9

Check this out!
When I get exceptionally good service, I am likely to tell others.

Yes	97.0%
No	3.0

And finally . . .
How many instances of poor service does it take for you to change service providers?

1	16.9%
2	40.6
3	28.0
4 or more	14.3

(1.4 percent are absolutely masochistic. It takes 10 or more instances to get their attention! See? Even crummy operations can have at least a few customers . . . the slow learners!)

What do we see? Customers seem to be willing to accept quite a bit of responsibility for getting good customer service. After all, they're servers too! And wouldn't it be interesting to offer a customer training program so that customers could learn to help us serve them better?

3

THINK LIKE A CUSTOMER

We were flying in the soup at 9,000 feet, Buns and I, on our way to Cincinnati. We had been in Philadelphia on a speaking engagement and, after a late start, wanted to land at picturesque Lunken Field, where we would meet friends for dinner.

That was the plan. And you know what happens to plans.

First was the matter of a headwind right on our nose howling at about 40 knots and turning our normally fast single-engine plane into a real snoozer. Then came thunderstorms arcing from just south of Indianapolis all the way to Dayton and moving quickly east. Swell!

We calculated arrival times and had our fingers crossed that we could beat the storms to Cincy. Just for grins I dialed up WLW radio to get an on-the-spot perspective and was chilled to hear that tornado sirens were already blaring across the City of Seven Hills.

"Mooney niner-five-mike-kilo, Indy Center." The air traffic control center in Indianapolis was calling.

"Go ahead, Indy."

"I'm showing level three and some level four at your 12 o'clock and about three-zero miles. Also Dayton is reporting a line of level four thunderstorms just over the airport. Say your intentions."

This is one of those duh moments. I wanted to land!

"We'd like to amend our destination to Wilmington." I had stabbed my finger at the map and landed on Wilmington, Ohio. The only thing special about Wilmington was that it wasn't straight ahead and it wasn't in Dayton.

"Turn 30 right, descend, and maintain 5,000."

"Wilco, five-mike-kilo."

Buns and I scrambled for the charts. We had never landed in Wilmington but the en route charts said it had plenty of runway and an instrument approach that we'd need as the sky turned from dull white to somber gray and then was sucked into a black hole that started just the other side of our windscreen. I flipped on the navigation lights, as if that would matter.

"Five-mike-kilo, have you gotten permission to use Wilmington?" The calm voice from Indy was back in our headphones.

"Negative." I was puzzled as this was unusual. So I added, "Do I need to?"

"I got it for you. Turn another ten to the right and expect ILS runway two-six-right."

It turned out that Wilmington is the private airport owned by Airborne Express, and it was under no obligation to entertain unexpected company. But as the lightning began to split the darkness off our left wingtip, a long ribbon of white lights winked on just ahead and a bit to the right. Red runway end identification lights marked the beginning of the concrete strip that would save us, and bright white rabbit lights flashed in a sequence that pulled us closer.

Unseen radio beacons reached up from the rain-soaked farmland below and signaled the autopilot until it locked on and began to send our little plane down an invisible rail that ended in the runway.

"Niner-five-mike-kilo, contact tower . . . "

"Tower, Mooney niner-five-mike-kilo on the glide slope two-six-left."

"Five-mike-kilo, you are cleared to land. Winds are two-four-zero at 16 gusting to 28. We're sending a van to marshall you to the ramp. Look for the flashing lights when you clear."

Once on the ground, we were met with umbrellas and a ride to the employee cafeteria, where we waited out the storm, fired back up, and launched into the clear, smooth air behind the storm floating gently into Cincinnati, good friends, and a great dinner.

Here's the question: What were they thinking?

What was the controller in Indy Center thinking when he vectored a small airplane to a private field just minutes ahead of a killer storm?

What was the tower controller thinking when she opened a closed airfield and sent a security officer to ensure that an unexpected aircraft was ushered quickly to shelter and unexpected guests offered comfort in a raging storm?

They were thinking like customers.

The controller could have left it to us to discover that Wilmington was a private field. He could have left it to us to try to raise the tower by radio. Could have but didn't. Instead, he anticipated our needs and called via landline to secure permission.

And how about the tower controller? Airborne Express Field is usually open only in the wee hours of the morning when the big jets of Airborne return to nest and trade packages with one another in the massive distribution center that dominates midfield. The tower controller could have easily declined. But she didn't. Instead, she anticipated our needs and treated us like customers.

Okay, here's a fair question: How in the world do you get management and employees to think like a customer? I have four steps:

1. Sample your own service.
2. Learn to listen.
3. Check out the other guys, the competition.
4. Hire customer contemporaries.

SAMPLE YOUR SERVICE

How did you feel the last time you went to a restaurant and needed help making your selection? Or when you asked the server about the soup of the day or the dinner special, and the best he could do was recite the basic ingredients? How did you feel when you were told, "We aren't allowed to eat that dish, but my customers tell me it's very good. I highly recommend it!"

Bull!

Or how about the recorded message that advises, "This call may be monitored for training or quality assurance purposes. Please hold for the next available representative."

I'll bet you know what's coming. Exactly who should be monitoring the calls? A supervisor waiting to say, "Gotcha!" or should it be someone else?

Would hotel housekeepers turn room thermostats to subzero if just once they checked a room and discovered that it was cold enough to hang fresh meat? And just as aggravating, would they appreciate being awakened at an ungodly hour because the housekeeper failed to unset the alarm clock?

Would an apartment owner tolerate bugs in the kitchen if he had to live there? I think not!

And here's an easy one. Would the leadership of most major corporations allow those god-awful voice messaging systems if the only way they could call their own office was to use them?

"To speak to your administrative assistant, say or press one. To access your voice mail, enter your last name followed by your mother's maiden name by using the touch tone keys or press pound followed by an ampersand to hold for an attendant . . . "

Mystery. Sometimes it's just not possible to sample your own service. No problem, have someone do it for you! Hire a mystery shopping service, but be careful to follow the guidelines below or the only thing that may be shopped is your wallet! I asked Vickie Henry of Feedback Plus, perhaps the best mystery shopper I know, for advice on selecting the right mystery shopping service.

Hiring the right service isn't a matter of cruising the Yellow Pages. Begin by determining what you wish to accomplish with the service. Mystery shopping is much too involved and valuable to waste the investment creating a third-party gotcha!

Vickie says, "Begin with a measure of baseline performance. To measure the value of the program, you have to have a starting point.

"Select a service with first-rate technological expertise. This will improve the accuracy of the reports, speed the delivery of the reports, and be of major value when it's time to interpret the data gathered."

A good shopper service will be able to create a survey tool targeted specifically for you and—this is important—provide ample shoppers to meet your specific needs. Vickie added that it's critical the service you hire has enough shoppers so they aren't "busted" by your crew.

Plan on incorporating shopper reports directly into your training program. You'll want a service that knows how to turn raw data into tips for training. And to mine especially useful data, you may want a shopper service with the ability to offer real-time data.

One terrific use for a shopper service is the provision of immediate, positive feedback. For example, a shopper at a fast-food franchise might deliver an on-the-spot reward if the server remembers to suggest a menu special.

Vickie advises that when choosing a mystery shopper service, you should do the following:

- Look for a company that has a proven track record.
- Choose a member of MSPA, Mystery Shopping Providers Association.
- Get at least three testimonials from past and present clients.
- Ask for a trial shopping period.
- Ask for sample reporting choices and make sure the results of the one you select has user-friendly interpretations.
- Last, but not least, ask for a profile of shoppers—how many, their demographics, and how they are certified, rated, and scheduled.

I figured Vickie would have at least one story of the "What were they thinking?" variety. This was her reply:

"The one I'm best known for, Scott, I always share in my Would You Do Business with You? seminars.

"We always instruct our shoppers to allow plenty of time for the server to offer dessert. This can be hundreds of thousands of dollars on the bottom line for a restaurant chain if every server suggested desserts. In Tallahassee, Florida, a Feedback shopper was in a fine dining restaurant, where the server had not offered dessert. Our shopper finally said, "I believe I'll have a dessert tonight." The young lady looked at him and said, "Are you kidding? After all you just ate!"

"Here's one I heard last week. A young shopper was in a large, upscale department store. She wears a size 6 and, according to her, is built a little like Jennifer Lopez. The sales associate was helping her select slacks to go with a silk blouse when the associate jovially and somewhat loudly commented, "Ahhh . . . Baby's got 'back'!"

> **T** *h i n k i n g* **P** *o i n t*
>
> *How could you . . . and your team sample your service?*

LEARN TO LISTEN

We do what we do because we think it will get us what we want. Humans are organisms in search of positive consequences. We act and then watch to see what our behavior brings: Good results yield more; poor results usually get less of the associated behavior.

Insanity is sometimes defined as repeating the same behavior but expecting a different result with each repeat. Maybe management insanity should be defined as expecting employees to change without feedback.

Take, for example, one definition of tips, a form of feedback that is the basic pay of servers, bartenders, and even the guy who delivers your newspaper. Some say it stands for "ensuring prompt service." A tip is feedback, pure and simple. Lay a five-dollar bill on the edge of your table in a restaurant, and watch what happens to service. But divorce the consequence from the behavior, such as the case when the tip is automatically tacked onto the bill, and then watch what happens to service. *Feedback,* another word for consequence, drives performance.

Almost as bad as no feedback is feedback so long in coming that it becomes disconnected to the behavior. And that's the good news! When an employee is finally presented with *delayed* feedback, the behavior it reconnects to is totally unrelated behavior!

We know a child who was slow being potty trained. It turned out his parents made the child sit in the bathroom alone when he misbehaved. Naturally, he soon associated the bathroom with punishment!

What we know so far is that *effective feedback should be immediate and associated with the behavior.* One more key ingredient: *the quality of the feedback.* Here's where learning to listen pays off.

Let's say a server gives poor service, but the customer still leaves a good tip. What is the lesson learned? Any service is good service. Now let's say a server gives poor service, and the customer leaves neither tip nor explanation. The lesson learned? Some customers are cheap!

But now let's say a server gives poor service, receives a poor tip along with a comment card that says, "Service was slow, there was no refill of my coffee, and the server refused to substitute an English muffin for the toast." Now the lesson *can* be learned!

Listening is different from hearing. Listening implies that there is a certain quality to the feedback received. Great managers give detailed feedback regularly and create systems that help employees do more than simply hear customers—they help them listen!

CHECK OUT THE OTHER GUYS

One of the best ways to encourage employees to think like a customer is to let them become customers—of your competition! If it's difficult sometimes to criticize yourself, it's easy to take a poke at the other guy.

Stew Leonard of grocery fame used to pile his department heads into a van and go idea shopping at the competition. Stew Jr. told me that the goal was to find one good idea every trip. "Good finding" is a nice idea, but "bad finding" works even better.

Take your crew to the competition and invite them to rip the competitors apart. It's nothing more than human nature at work to find things wrong with the other guy. The good news is that the exercise makes it much easier to see the two-by-four in your own eye once you've discovered that the competition has a speck of dust in theirs. Give your folks clipboards and tape recorders, stopwatches and thermometers, and turn them loose. Then trot them home and turn them loose on one another. Boy, are you about to see a cat fight!

For added benefit, take your employees to nonrelated businesses for a bit of what engineers call "parallel analysis." This is the practice of observing folks with similar problems in dissimilar industries. Where do you think hoteliers got the idea for their customer loyalty programs? From the airlines, which got the idea from fast-food restaurants, which I believe got the idea from dry cleaners.

Good ideas don't care where they come from, but you have to be willing to fetch!

> ### T h i n k i n g   P o i n t
>
> *Where could you discover ideas to improve your service?*

HIRE CUSTOMER CONTEMPORARIES

Nordstrom started it. Home Depot and Lowes picked up the tune. It makes great sense to hire contemporaries of your customers. It takes someone who knows plumbing to sell plumbing to plumbers just as surely as one fashionista can recognize another.

Southwest Airlines plays a variation of the theme when it invites frequent-flier customers to assist with interviewing future flight attendants. The theory is that customers should know best which candidate has the potential to wow another customer.

> ### T h i n k i n g   P o i n t
>
> *Where could you go to hire customer contemporaries? How could you*
> *invite customers to share their viewpoints in a positive way?*

4

THE FOUR ELEMENTS OF CUSTOMER SERVICE

Customer service is one of the few products manufactured on the spot, one customer at a time. Give me any corporate slogan you want or flash the coolest mission statement in the world, but you aren't going to change the fact that at the moment of service, that so-called moment of truth, four elements come together that affect the kind of service that this customer in this unrepeatable moment of time is going to get. Good or bad, fast or slow, attentive or totally indifferent—you can't take it back. You might fix it, but that will be after the fact.

The four elements that influence the service experience are the server, the boss, the customer, and the environment. Let's look at the elements separately.

THE SERVER

No matter how well you train or how many details you engineer into the system, the server has choices. A server can choose to give you a world-class experience or make you absolutely miserable. And most of the time these extremes fall within company policy. Maybe no policy is intended to allow such variation, but most often it does.

One late night I raced through DFW Airport to catch an American Airlines flight home. Hot, sweaty, loosened tie flapping, I practically dove onto the plane. As I panted past the flight attendant, I smiled and said, "When you get a chance, how about a vanilla shake for 11B?" (We're talking coach, not first class.)

I was being funny, so you can imagine my surprise when seconds after being seated, the flight attendant appeared at my seat holding a glass goblet of vanilla ice cream! For some reason the cabin lights were off, but nonetheless I could see she was smiling.

"We didn't have the shake, but this was extra and I thought you might enjoy it!"

And I'm not even cute! See? Servers have choices. I bet a zillion dollars that nowhere in the AA training manual is there mention of what to do in this situation.

A friend of mine couldn't wait to tell me about the day he visited a national home center in search of a special air filter. When he asked the first clerk he spotted where he might find such a filter, the clerk, without so much as looking up, simply said, "We don't have them."

What the clerk didn't say but could have said was, "That particular filter is out of season. We should have them in a couple of weeks." He could have said but did not say, "If you'd like to leave your name and number, I'll be happy to call when they come in. And if you can't wait that long, I can call the manufacturer to have them shipped direct to you."

Could have but didn't. Servers have choices.

We took a break from writing and headed for the grocery. Company was coming, and they have been asking for Buns's famous pork spare ribs. (See the Appendix for the recipe; they are to die for!) At the store I was dispatched to the meat counter while Buns selected flowers for the guest room.

"Sir, do you have more pork spare ribs in the back? There are none in the display case. I'd like a nice big one, please."

The butcher nodded and disappeared into the cooler. In less than a minute he rematerialized carrying a large box labeled Montfort Meats that contained probably a dozen Cryovac packages of ribs.

The first package hit the scale; a label was printed and pasted to the plastic package. Up came another set of ribs for a repeat performance; there was another and another. And I got the idea that this guy was on a roll! As long as I was willing to stand there and watch, he was just going to label them all!

"Sir, I only need one."

Plop! Plastic and pork flopped onto the counter.
What was he thinking?

THE BOSS

I believe that great hiring trumps indifferent leadership. In the real world, where we have minimally trained marginal hires, leadership has a disproportionate impact on the quality of customer service.

And a tremendously valuable asset is going to waste in your organization—face time. Face time is that old real estate principle of highest and best use applied to the boss.

Face time is important for three reasons: status, example, and intelligence.

Office time almost never has the same value as face time. Offices are too often a place to hide. If the boss has superior expertise, he or she should be in the field or on the floor where it can be shared, leading by example.

When the boss is in direct contact with customers, face time has incredible value. When we owned our little restaurant, people wanted to be recognized by the owner. They wanted to know that when they walked in the door, the owner—not a clerk, a cook, or an assistant—would call them by name. Think about the businesses that make you feel good, and I guarantee that the boss is likely to be present much of the time.

You visit the White House. What do your neighbors want to know? See what I mean? The same goes for your business. Your customers want to see Y-O-U!

Face time also has immeasurable value in terms of training. The things your people are most likely to do (learn) are the things that they see in the work environment and try for themselves. Like it or not, what the boss does, the troops do. Boss grouchy; troops grouchy. Boss quality minded; troops watch quality. Boss cleans break room; boss cleans break room! (This stuff is powerful but not perfect!!)

The third value of face time is intelligence gathering. All of the mystery shoppers, 800 lines, comment cards, and focus groups in the world won't tell you half as much as will your loyal customers. Nothing beats asking customers face-to-face what they like about your product or service or how they would change it if they were in charge. Customers will help you beat your competition if they think they are dealing with someone who can and will make a change for the better.

T *h i n k i n g*   **P** *o i n t*

How could you get more face time with customers and employees?

THE CUSTOMER

A paramedic I know is one of the best in the business. He can start an IV line in the back of an ambulance flying down a rough ranch road, and chances are the patient won't even notice.

One rather gory scene I worked involved a family of five driving a minivan and one very drunk loser almost driving a pickup truck. Mom had minor injuries but Dad and the kids were hurt pretty bad. As luck would have it, the drunk was more drunk than hurt, but protocol required that he be fitted with a C collar, and secured to a backboard with an IV line started as a precaution against his condition deteriorating. My paramedic friend took one look at the drunk, thought about the family he had nearly obliterated, stripped open the IV kit, and predicted, "This may hurt a little." And it did.

Customers have more influence over service received than you might imagine.

One late night when I had managed to get within 300 miles and a short flight from home, fog had settled over Houston like a dark, wet blanket, and no one was going anywhere. I set off in search of a room and was told that within ten miles of the airport there were exactly . . . none.

No problem. I stopped at the nearest hotel, ignored the completely full parking lot, walked up to the counter, and said to the clerk (who looked like she had been rode hard and put up wet), "Would you happen to have room for just one skinny guy? I was six foot six and gorgeous when I left home this morning and now look at me!" She smiled just a teensy bit. You could tell no one had taken her out to play in more than a day, so I continued, "If it would help, I can look pitiful. How's this?" I gave her my best hangdog look; her smile inched beyond a crack but wasn't yet the grin I was going for. "I think you can do better than that." She was catching the spirit. I went from pitiful to "pitifuller" if there is such a thing.

"I don't have any rooms but so you don't have to get any shorter, I'm going to put you in a suite right above the lobby. It's set for a conference in the morning, and it only has a Murphy bed. If you won't sleep until noon, I'll give it to you for the price of a single."

Bingo! Room! Discount! Happy!

Don't tell me customers don't influence the service they receive in a big way. Later I'll show you exactly how. For now, be aware that customers have a lot more control than they expect.

> **T** h i n k i n g **P** o i n t
>
> *What could you do to positively influence the service you get?*

THE ENVIRONMENT

Last Friday a line of monster storms marched the length of our quiet valley, still green in October following a summer of record precipitation. As beautiful as storms can be, they often spawn unexpected consequences. (Was it W. C. Fields who said, "Thunder is impressive, but it's the lightning that does the work"?) Lightning did a number on our phone system and fried line two. No problem. We have plenty of phone lines.

The storms dragged behind them the first cold front of the season, dropping temperatures a quick 20 degrees. The sultry southerly winds were replaced by gusting winds out of the north that packed enough wind chill to freeze our Texas hides.

We called the phone company and, unlike big city utilities, our repairman was out in an instant. He was so quick we suspected he had been waiting at the local Mini Mart in case we called. He should have gone home to get a jacket, because there stood our repairman outside the office door with the wind whipping his shirt, causing him to shift impatiently from one freezing foot to the other while digging around in the junction box in search of the problem. After 10 or 15 cold minutes, he appeared red-faced at the office door and announced, "Everything on our side of the box checks out just fine. It looks like it's in your system. Sorry about that."

Before he could jump into his truck to leave, Buns called me from the other side of the office as the only available reinforcement to hold him. Fifteen even colder minutes later, we (the repairman and I) had located the problem and made the fix, and an even frostier repair guy was headed back to the Mini Mart for another shot of coffee.

"Buns, if it had been ten degrees warmer, or his wife had sent him to work with a jacket, we would have gotten better service."

Water, Please!

There's more to the environment than wind chill. The environment includes equipment, available space, and time to do the work properly. It even includes the influence of culture.

I love Germany and Germans, but ask them for a glass of ice water and you are more likely to die of thirst than be served. Our first trip to Europe had me asking for *wasser, berg wasser, kuchen wasser, wasser wasser.* *"Ich mochte wasser, keine gasse, bitte."* (I want water without gas, please.) It didn't matter. They would bring me bottled carbonated water if they brought me anything at all.

The Brits and the Dutch weren't much better, although I did find a place in London called the Texas Embassy Cantina, where they brought me a pitcher of iced tea. And the Pizza Hut in Heidelberg served me a huge glass of ice water that actually had plenty of ice. I could have kissed them on the lips. (I offered!)

Does this mean that service in Europe is awful? No, it just demonstrates that culture influences the way servers hear you. They neither expect nor understand a request that is foreign to them. Keep in mind that anything that is not familiar to you could rightfully be labeled foreign. In North Dakota I once ordered jalapenos for my baked potato. That didn't work, so I said, "I'll be happy if you bring me a bottle of Tabasco." In a few minutes the server warily placed a bottle of Tabasco on the table and said, "We had a bottle in the bar. I don't think anyone has ever used this stuff."

In State College, Pennsylvania, we ordered the spicy Three Mile Island version of hot wings at Hooters. "Are you sure?" asked the server, looking at us as if we were from Mars instead of Texas. "I've never taken an order for this before." After serving our extra-spicy wings, she checked back several times. Instead of asking if the food was alright, she asked, "Are *you* alright?"

And that's how we brought Texas culture to State College!

Rock, Paper, Scissors

What we don't know—and have made no attempt to discover—is exactly which of the service elements is the most important. We think, but again don't know, that the weight of each element is situational.

For now, think of the relationship between the service elements as similar to kids playing rock, paper, scissors. Do you know this routine? You and your partner start with hands together in a gentle clasp. You chant "rock, paper, scissors" while bringing your hands together in a silent clap for the first two beats. On the third beat you bring the raised hand into the palm of the other hand, only this time it falls as a fist (rock), a flat hand (paper), or two open fingers (scissors). To determine who wins the round, the rules are that rock smashes scissors, scissors cut paper, and paper wraps rock. Sometimes rock wins and sometimes not; the same is true for the other two. It depends on the combination.

And that's the way it is with the elements of service. Great hiring beats poor leadership; great customers overcome poor servers; and great leaders can inspire mediocre team members. All of these contribute to the environment in which the service product will flourish or perish.

Read on and I'll show you exactly how to line up the elements of service in your favor so none of your customers will walk away saying, "What were they thinking?"

> **T** h i n k i n g **P** o i n t
>
> *What policies or elements of the physical environment are*
> *causing a negative influence on service at your place?*

5

INFLUENCES ON THE
SERVICE ENVIRONMENT

Afeature article in *Time* magazine
(14 Oct. 2000) asserted this to be the crisis in American education:
nearly one in two college freshmen require remedial courses in English
or math. A second feature article in the same issue reported a trend
toward bigger houses, an odd trend as families are getting smaller, not
larger. Do you think this news has anything to do with the quality of job
applicants or the way today's employee must be managed? It does!

I cite *Time* only because it is on my desk. My dollar says you can
open your morning newspaper (if you are among the dwindling number of Americans who still read a paper) and discover similar anecdotal
evidence that today's workers are going to be very different from their
parents.

By the way, newspapers went to almost every house on the block in
1950. Thanks to morning and evening papers serving the same market,
the subscription rate was 160 percent. Today, only 57 percent of American households find a newspaper on their doorstep. If employees
seem ignorant—they are! The landmark midterm elections of 2002 saw
one of the lowest voter participation rates in history. (Fewer votes were
cast in a national election than were cast for the first *American Idol* competition!)

Are the two *Time* articles related? I think so.

One *Time* reader responded in the June 10, 2002, edition by writing, "The real problem is the poor educational standards in high schools that make these remedial college courses necessary." In response to the article on housing trends, another wrote that "this new American home is not about family cohesion but about accommodating different lifestyles"; yet another wrote, "These new homes look beautiful but I couldn't spot a single bookcase."

Ask any business owner or department manager, and they will tell you that increasingly the boss must act as parent to ill-educated, poorly mannered young people. Whoops! I take that back. I should have said poorly mannered *people*. Want evidence?

Go to the theatre and notice how many folks, young and old, answer their cell phone after treating us to a chorus of annoying phone music. Attend any conference and listen to the folks in front of you chatting away.

And you can't figure why your employees don't naturally say "Yes, sir" and "No, ma'am." It's a cultural thing and it isn't good. A recent poll by cellmanners.com revealed that 60 percent of us would like to ban cell phones from live performances, and even more (about 65 percent) think they have no place in church. Fine, but look at the numbers who think it's perfectly fine to interrupt a play or a prayer for a quick chat with the office!

What this means to the boss is that training must extend beyond the procedural how-to. Effective customer service training has to include basic manners.

> **T** *h i n k i n g* **P** *o i n t*
>
> *What cultural issues should be added to your training program?*

UNDER THE INFLUENCE

If you wonder what is influencing employee behavior, maybe you should turn on television.

Start with a look at the characters in television commercials. In the '50s we had Betty Crocker, the Jolly Green Giant, Aunt Jemima, and the Marlboro Man. Today's TV characters with top-of-mind rating are McGruff the Crime Prevention Dog, the Crash Test Dummies, and the Dell Dude.

Betty Crocker has been replaced by parents who think box cutters are kitchen appliances. And bright green ketchup is now the vegetable equivalent of Green Giant vegetables. The Marlboro Man we don't miss mainly because the number-one movie the week this was written was *Jackass.*

The number-one song in the '50s was by Gene Autry. Go ahead, guess. It was *Rudolph the Red-Nosed Reindeer. White Christmas* by Bing Crosby was number two. A half century later kids were tapping their feet to *The Thong Song* by Sisgo and *Oops! I Did It Again* by Britney Spears.

Because we had no MTV in the '50s, you'll have to use your imagination to get a picture of the *Rudolph* and *White Christmas* videos. For *The Thong Song* and the number by Ms. Britney, no imagination is required.

Just for fun take a look at the Top Ten Jingles of the Twentieth Century (rated as most memorable) and notice how many are from the last decade . . . or not:

1. You deserve a break today. (McDonald's)
2. Be all that you can be. (U.S. Army)
3. Pepsicola hits the spot.
4. M'm, m'm! Good! (Campbells)
5. See the USA in your Chevrolet. (G.M.)
6. I wish I was an Oscar Meyer weiner.
7. Double your pleasure, double your fun. (Wrigley's Doublemint Gum)
8. Winston tastes good like a cigarette should.
9. It's the real thing. (Coca-Cola)
10. Brylcream . . . a little dab'll do ya.

In the '50s and '60s our national icons were Charlie Tuna, Mr. Whipple, and Mr. Clean. Today they are P Diddy (formerly Puff Daddy), Eminem, and Cedric the Entertainer.

In the '60s Sugar Pops were tops and Smokey Bear was reminding us that only we could prevent forest fires.

Today the top-selling video game is Grand Theft Auto where you can hire the services of a prostitute, murder her, and take her money as your reward. Dude! You're getting a Dell!

In 1950 the average hourly wage was $1.29, and the annual household income was $3,216. By 2000 the average wage was $13.64 per hour and the average household income $23,927—in 1950 dollars. (The actual average household income is $41,994.) Of course, you have to adjust for taxes paid and somehow figure the value of government services received. But in a few words, we're much better off financially.

In 1950 the average family had 6 children. By 2000 that number had dropped to 1.8, and the number of single-parent households quadrupled (from 4.5 percent to 18.5 percent), according to the U.S. Census Bureau!

> **T**h i n k i n g   **P**o i n t
>
> *If today's employees are different, doesn't it stand to reason that training and leadership must also change?*

Boomers Say Bye

When does 70 million minus 40 million equal zero? When you are looking at the labor force of the United States over the next couple of decades! This was one of those factoids on the front cover of *USA Today* that graphically told the story of an aging boomer population and the impact of its members' retirement on the available workforce. Nice graph, wrong interpretation.

The graph leads easily to the conclusion that 40 million new entrants into the labor force won't nearly cover the jobs vacated by retiring boomers. Although the math is correct, the conclusion doesn't quite measure up. The assumption is that there will be 70 million holes to fill. I doubt it.

It *is* true that the post–World War II baby boom population is slowly working its way through its life cycle. First was the impact on delivery rooms and maternity wards followed by a sudden shortage of classroom space and teachers. Then we did our thing in the '60s, grew up, and went to work with each successive phase of our life having a noticeable impact on everything from music to insurance rates. Now, we are gray but not yet gone, and the demographers are already filling our places with Gen Xers and Gen Yers.

But what won't be filled are the holes we'll leave in the workforce, not because we boomers are irreplaceable, but because we will no longer be necessary. (This trend has already begun and is misinterpreted as a sign of an ailing economy. Wrong. It is the sign of a healthy economy in transition.) Why? Because as George Carlin once said, "We don't need any more stuff. We have our stuff." America and most of the developed world is awash in stuff.

At our house our stuff cup runneth over. You bring new stuff in; you gotta take some old stuff out. We have no more room for stuff. Too much stuff. Too much inexpensive stuff. When it is too easy to produce or outsource new stuff, what are you left with? More stuff!

And that's why there's no need to fully replace the boomers who are about to sign off. Forty million new workers may be more than what is needed to replace the boomers to keep us sated with stuff. George Orwell wrote in his landmark book *1984* about a society in which the mantra was "better end than mend." He was ahead of his time.

THE SERVICE EXPERIENCE: THE REAL CHALLENGE

Two things are almost certain to happen that will influence how and what Americans will be served. First, as we become ever more efficient at producing stuff, stuff will become cheaper and, I probably should add, better. It is likely that products bought today will be obsolete long before they wear out.

As a case in point, I remember my grandparents saving to buy a color television. The front of the cabinet had spaces for several knobs for adjusting color and contrast. And, of course, there was the ever-popular horizontal hold. (If you are under 30, you'll need to look that one up in a dictionary.)

My grandma and grandpa's color set (which cost more than the car my dad was driving at the time) was purchased at a furniture store and delivered to the house, where a repairman had to do the initial setup. Oh, yes, they also purchased the option of new rabbit ears (set-top antenna). (Better not put the dictionary away just yet!) Today we can buy a bigger, better set that needs little or no installation for a fraction of the cost. Stuff is getting better and cheaper.

When I did some fence work down along the north property line, the repair called for a drill, so I carried a lightweight 18-volt cordless model that cost not a penny more than the metal-cased corded anchor that my dad had bought on credit several decades ago.

Better and cheaper stuff is turning specialty items into commodities; and all because technology and engineering have enabled fewer workers to produce more in less time. When Volkswagen first appeared, it took the factory crew 30 minutes to install the engine. Today the engine in the new Beetle slips in, in just over 3 minutes. Better stuff, faster. In 1950 a Sears corded drill weighed 21 pounds and cost about $70, a fortune in those times. Today Craftsman offers a lighter 8.5 pounds as their heaviest and better drill for fewer bucks!

Customers have learned there are some products for which there is no useful service component, like toilet paper. Those products you buy at Sam's or Costco. And you can't buy products wholesale for what Mr. Sam can sell 'em retail. That's the bad news (for the retailer), and it only gets worse.

Smart manufacturers are learning how to produce sophisticated products with the knowledge component already built in. We bought a cheap TV at Wal-Mart, and once installed in our bathroom (I said cheap!), the set immediately went into setup mode when first turned on. It walked me through a brief installation process, and before you could say "shower and shave," our favorite channels were programmed. Do I need an electronic sales specialist? Not even. Sell it to me cheap, and let the product itself provide the details.

Here's why smart service providers are going to focus on the experience. Wal-Mart is poised to double its sales in the next five years. Is that significant? You bet it is! Wal-Mart is the 800-pound gorilla that wants to sit next to you! Wal-Mart will create 800,000 new jobs in the United States in the next half decade. It is already putting SuperCenters as close as five miles apart and then backfilling with smaller grocery-convenience stores called the Neighborhood Market!

An astonishing 25 percent of the entire United States economy's productivity improvement between 1995 and 1999 was the result of efficiency gains at one company—Wal-Mart. Here's what Wal-Mart wants to do: be everywhere it isn't, and that's more than just geography. Wal-Mart says it wants at least 30 percent market share in any business it's in.

Jack Welch used to promote the idea that GE should be number one or number two in any industry it was in. That was a pretty big threat but only if you produced such high-tech items as jet engines and nuclear power plants. When Wal-Mart makes such a claim, you have to worry if you are selling used cars or Christian books.

What will be left to sell?

Experience.

BETTER, CHEAPER, LASTS FOREVER

In the barn is a Sears Craftsman scroll saw. It was an expensive gift in 1972. Amortized over three decades, you'd have to admit it was a pretty good investment. My guess is that it will still be sawing long after I've turned to dust.

Also in the barn are the shipping cartons for the three VHS tape players in our house. I kept them in case I had to return them for repairs—a bad idea. A new VHS VCR costs less than an hour of a technician's time. When the VCR goes, it will go completely—into the dumpster!

In 1980, 1.1 percent of United States households had VCRs. By 1990, it was 72 percent; just about all who were going to buy had bought. Introduced by Sony in 1975 at a price of $1,600, the venerable entertainment machine could be purchased today at an everyday Wal-Mart low price of 60 bucks. Why? DVD has arrived.

If you're working in a factory where they make only VCRs, it's time to shop the résumé. It's not that VCRs have failed. It's quite the opposite. VCRs are products that have succeeded spectacularly. But everyone who might want a VCR has a VCR. Now they are done, finished, toast. It's time to make way for the next new thing.

What happened to the VCR may be happening to the desktop computer, travel-sized hair dryers, CD players, even irons and ironing boards. The Sharper Image is selling an electric nose hair trimmer! Once all of us who have nose hairs get trimmed, The Sharper Image will have to go looking for the next big thing.

Acknowledging that products will become cheaper and better brings us to point number two. As products come and go with increasingly shorter lifecycles, the need for workers with specific skills will increase exponentially.

The future will have two types of workers: service workers and knowledge workers. The knowledge workers will have but one specialized ability, the ability to learn new tasks and technologies on a regular basis. The service workers, at least the successful ones, will be masters at providing a service experience.

There may even be room for an all-new career: a customer experience engineer. Even manufactured products will require ever more clever customer service and experience components. From customer service help lines to customer affinity programs to bells and whistles intended to add value, a whole host of service and experience elements will slow a product's slide to commodity status.

BETTER, CHEAPER, FASTER CUSTOMER SERVICE

What we are saying is that better, cheaper, faster no longer governs manufacturing only; it now applies to customer service. The folks who figure out how to provide a killer service experience (we call it Positively Outrageous Service) better, cheaper, and faster than the competition will rule the market.

The complicating factor is that 70 million minus 40 million equals zero. It's quite possible that as technology continues to leave Americans awash in stuff, fewer jobs will be in manufacturing and more jobs in the service industry. We'll probably have all the bodies we'll need to run the economy, but will they be the right kind of bodies? Will they have the psychological makeup that service employers will need to be service competitive?

Read on and we'll show you how to avoid being left behind.

> ### T h i n k i n g   P o i n t
> *How could you increase the knowledge content of your*
> *product and the experience content of your service?*

6

DIVE INTO THE
LABOR POOL

The first candidate through the door has the look of a winner. If you're like most of us, you are an excellent judge of character, and the interview is nothing more than an opportunity for you to talk about the company and yourself and perhaps spend a few moments to verify your first impression. Am I right?

Wrongo rio!

In the customer service business, first impressions are a huge deal because few service transactions last longer than a first impression. Even though a great first impression is a must, you want the interview to last long enough for you to be certain you've made the right selection. And you will never, ever be certain based solely on a first impression.

Why? Try these interesting stats in the archives of Monster.com on for size (probably not statistically reliable but certainly indicative; visit Monster.com and see for yourself):

- Twenty-four percent of the respondents admit to having lied on a résumé.
- When asked to rank family, money, and career in order of importance, is there any doubt which came in a poor third place? (In case you are dense, family was ranked as most important by 72 percent. A whopping 16 percent thought money was most impor-

tant, whereas all of 10 percent put career at the head of the list.) Boss, when an employee is faced with a crisis at work or at home, sorry, pal, you lose.

- Only 45 percent say they respect their boss, and about 40 percent report they have a great relationship with their boss. Guess where that leaves the rest of them? Another 35 percent say their relationship with the boss is nonexistent!
- If they tell you in the interview they left their last job because they were unhappy, well, that may be true. A fat 75 percent of American workers say they would settle for lower pay to be happier at work, although you can pretty much factor out minimum-wage earners who haven't had a raise in years. They're struggling to pay the rent. To heck with happiness!

THE BEST HIRE

The best hire is the great employee you already have. When we owned our restaurant, I am proud to say we *never* hung the banner of shame—Help Wanted. Why? Because we rarely lost employees. Why? Because people don't leave jobs they love, and they love jobs where they are loved.

Hanging a Help Wanted sign can be translated into customer terms as "Don't come in here. We don't have sufficient staff and you haven't a prayer of getting served." In terms of job seekers, Help Wanted signs are often translated as "No one wants to work here. You'd have to be a desperate idiot to apply."

Ann Rhoades of People, Inc., says, "You've got to rerecruit them every day." Her alma mater, Southwest Airlines, got the message in a big way. Following a highly successful Freedom to Fly ad campaign, the scrappy, profitable airline launched an *internal* Freedom to Fly campaign to pitch the benefits of *working* for Southwest.

Employee-targeted brochures urge Southwest team members to "Feel Free to Actually Enjoy What You Do" and reminds them that "You've Got the Freedom to Set Your Own Direction." Southwest Airlines University for People (catch the name!) established Career Development Services to actively assist employees in achieving their personal goals while remaining in the Southwest system.

Accomplishing personal goals through your job? Yes!!!

On its Web site, Monster.com asked visitors which New Year's resolutions they would be most likely to keep. A stunning 5 percent vowed to do better at the job they had, and a whopping 64 percent pledged to simply punch out and "find a new job."

> **T** h i n k i n g **P** o i n t
>
> *The best employee to recruit is the great employee you already have!*
> *Which of your employees need to be rerecruited?*

Here's one I'd rerecruit. From *Time* (28 Oct. 2002) comes the story of Johnny Bomaster, an employee of Southwest Airlines in Buffalo, New York. When Bomaster, a maintenance mechanic, looked out his window, all he saw was snow, nearly seven feet of the white stuff. One of the planes under Bomaster's care had been stuck so long that it was due for a routine maintenance check. No check, no fly. With Bomaster it would also be no problem. Tossing his toolbox on the back of his snowmobile, Bomaster rode the seven plus miles to the airport and started to work. By the next morning when the airport was flyable, so was the plane!

IT'S A GENERATIONAL THING

I have a ten-year-old pickup, which is old for a truck. I also have a ten-year-old grandson, not so old for a grandson. My grandson, Big Guy, stands all of 64¼ inches tall. (There are a series of marks on the bathroom wall where we have recorded his progress.) His granddad, Pops, has made it to his early 50s and can reach the Cheez-its on the top shelf without a boost.

Even though the Big Guy and I live on the same piece of Texas ranchland, in some respects we live on different planets. Sure, I'm the guy he wants to talk to when he has questions about baseball, science projects, and conflicts with his little sister. But there are other things that make the world look different to him, and it's not the perspective of being four-feet, six-and-a-quarter-inches tall. No, it's the age thing.

When I was in third grade, I very distinctly remember hearing Miss Allen tell us that a generation is 25 years. Every century you can count off four of them. But what was Gospel truth in 1958 is totally wrong today. Sociologists tell us that generations are no longer defined by the mere passage of time. A generation is defined by values and experiences, and they say our world is changing so fast that you can declare a new generation every four years. That's 25 to a century. My, how the world has changed since 1958! My, how the world has changed since yesterday!

Watching our favorite movie, *Sandlot,* the Big Guy rose up on one elbow and asked, "Pops, is there really a place called Sandlot and can you still get PF Flyers?" This from a kid who, while riding with me in that old pickup truck, asked, "Pops, how do you get the window down? This truck doesn't have any buttons!"

> **T** *h i n k i n g* **P** *o i n t*
>
> *The world is different, and if you are more than four or so years different in age from your employees, you had better give thought to how their values and experiences may influence their thoughts about work.*

HOW DIFFERENT ARE WE?

To begin, all Americans aren't white. Over 12 percent of Americans are black, more are Hispanic, and only 3.6 percent are Asian. But those percentages don't begin to describe our differences.

If you are black, you have only a one in three chance of living in a married couple household. A whopping 40 percent of black Americans are under the age of 24. If you are Hispanic, chances are your spending power is up; as a group your spending power has risen 315 percent in the past decade. Asian? Something's going on here! Although only 14 percent of Americans earn over $100,000, in the Asian community that number is 22 percent! Maybe that's because 44 percent of Asian adults have earned a bachelor's degree compared with 24 percent of the entire population.

The point is simple: You can't leave yourself at home. This is true whether you are the server or the served.

According to *USA Today,* 24 percent of Americans report they are chronically, not occasionally, angry at work. That's a lot of anger. A ton of us are disconnected from how we spend the bulk of our waking hours. According to authors Curt Coffman and Gabriel Gonzales-Molina in their book *Follow This Path* (Warner, 2002), "Only about one-third of the workplace in the United States is actively engaged, while approximately one-fifth is actively disengaged."

Check out *the cluetrain manifesto* at <www.cluetrain.com> for a better idea of how employees feel when they are customers:

> People of the earth . . . a powerful global conversation has begun. . . . Most corporations, on the other hand, only know how to talk in the soothing, humorless monotone of the mission statement, marketing brochure, and your-call-is-important-to-us busy signal. Same old tone, same old lies.

The radical signatories (Locke, Levine, Searles, and Weinberger) of the manifesto allege that corporations are afraid of the market, afraid of what they might hear if they really listened, and terrified at the prospect of allowing employees to communicate directly and freely with customers. (And God forbid that a company might encourage customers to talk to one another!)

Your employees bring these ideas with them when they come to work.

> **T** *h i n k i n g* **P** *o i n t*
>
> *How could you influence employees to feel a sense of ownership in their work and their company?*

Why Y?

Dr. Lane Longfellow is famous for saying, "You are what you were when." What he means is that the adult person you become is the child of the person you were. And if that needs interpretation, let's just say that the values and experiences of your youth determine the values carried into adulthood. (As I write this, Crosby, Stills, Nash, and Young are knocking out their hit song "Teach Your Children" on my CD player. How appropriate!)

The next generation to run the ship has been molded by its times and has become not so much Generation Y as Generation Why.

Nearly a quarter of Americans are Generation Y, born after 1979 and before 1994.

Eric Chester, who wrote *Employing Generation Why* (Chess Press, 2002), has a pretty good handle on what makes Gen Why tick. He says members of Gen Why have been shaped by the messages unique to their times: Why wait, why work, why pursue, why refrain, why aspire, and why abide.

Why Wait?

Who wants to wait? Who needs to wait when there is fast food and e-mail, and haven't you heard of FedEx? Serve Gen Y members or work with them, and the concept of waiting for lunch or a raise is totally foreign.

Why Work?

Buns and I ran into a former neighbor of high school age and were impressed to see him driving a late model Cadillac. Certain that the car was the product of hard work, frugal saving, and shrewd bargaining, we praised his great-looking wheels.

"Hey! Killer car! Bet you busted your chops for this one."

"Naw, my dad gave it to me."

"Yeah, well, it's still a good-looking ride, and I know keeping it insured and gassed has to take some effort."

"Not really."

"Not really?"

"Look," he turned to enunciate the new facts of life, saying, "you wouldn't give someone a Cadillac and not give them a credit card, would you?"

Why Pursue?

Before the dot-com implosion, tales abounded of recent college grads expecting huge salaries, a corner office, and flexible work schedules, all because they carried in their pockets a degree in computer science. No need to pursue when the world will come to you.

Why Refrain?

As this is being written, a few geniuses in San Francisco staged a "puke-in" by vomiting on the steps of City Hall as a statement that war makes them sick. This mid-50s writer has trouble committing the act to paper, but it's fair to ask why the Gen Y perpetrators should feel out of place when anything you could want to see—and a whole lot that you wouldn't—is as close as the remote control for the satellite TV.

Gen Yers have no need to save because there's no tomorrow. Ask them if they are concerned, and you'll be lucky if all you get is an "Are you nuts?" look. They weren't even born in 1973, and the concept of lines at gas stations because of gas rationing doesn't compute.

Why Aspire?

Even though I may not go along with the puke-in, I may have to agree with this next one. In a world that seems to have lost its collective sense of decency, maybe there isn't much reason to aspire. When entire societies adopt as their most noble calling strapping explosives around their waists in order to kill and maim as many innocents as possible, it's a fair question: Why aspire?

And that is the question Gen Y seems to be asking. Instead of aspiration, they settle for merely getting noticed, and perhaps this explains why Ozzie and Sharon Osborne have replaced Ozzie and Harriet Nelson.

Why Abide?

Why play by the rules when you can get away with flaunting them? In a society where even the "nice" kids rip and burn tunes from the Internet, why should shoplifting be too big an ethical leap?

Or how about these messages:

- No rules, just right!
- No Fear
- Just do it!
- No Boundaries

THE GOOD NEWS

Ask a boomer to describe a Gen Yer and you might hear "no common sense, no work ethic, no clue." But that would be wrong. For all their faults (boomers had none), Gen Yers have plenty to offer as long as it is offered on their terms.

They can be fiercely loyal, fast thinkers, and multitaskers, and they can edit (quickly separate out what is important to them) like there's no tomorrow. They adapt easily and thrive on change. Give them interesting work, recognition, and a chance to learn. Train them well—they hate looking stupid—and keep them informed. They aren't about to wear a dumb-looking uniform, and they aren't likely to want a rigid sales patter if they're willing to sell at all.

This is the first truly technofearless generation—but stay out of its way. Gen Yers eat when they are hungry and not by the clock!

Oh, and they do just fine with diversity, which is a good thing because the world no longer looks the way it did in 1958, which is also a good thing.

> **T** *h i n k i n g* **P** *o i n t*
>
> *How could you take advantage of Gen Y attitudes?*

X RATED!

If you're dealing with slightly older employees, you're dealing with Generation X. Born between 1965 and 1979, this generation looks entirely different from the one that followed it. This is a generation of entrepreneurs; even when they are employed, Gen Xers are highly entrepreneurial. As corporations are pushing teams, Gen Xers are not paying much attention. They are big on personal relationships and at the same time prefer fame over contentment two to one!

And whatever you say, chances are they don't believe it! Gen Xers are ad skeptics and pragmatists: "Life is tough, so what?" Chili's and Saturn have this generation tightly targeted: Get in, get out, get on with your life!

DIFFERENCES MATTER

If you let the Gen Yers chart us on Excel, this is how we might look:

Idea	Matures	Boomers	Xers	Yers
Defining	duty	individuality	diversity	self
Style	team player	self-absorbed	entrepreneur	so what?
Rewards	earned it	deserve it	need it	give it
Future	prepare	do it now	wait for it	what future?
Money	save	spend	hedge	spend
Meet	nightclubs	rock clubs	rave clubs	IM
Music	jazz	rock	alternative	everything
Stars	Sinatra	Beatles	Mariah Carey	Eminem

Idea	Matures	Boomers	Xers	Yers
Movies	Harlow	Mickey	J-Lo	Angelina
Heroes	Kilroy	Superman	Spiderman	Powerpuff girls
Tech	mimeo Kodak rotary party line	Xerox Polaroid Touch-Tone conference calls	desktop digital cell chat	CD DVD Wi-Fi IM
TV	boxing	Fantasy Island	Survivor	Bachelor
Auto	Packard	BMW	Saturn	PT Cruiser
Sex	wait	free love	protect yourself	wait?
Water	cistern	cooler	Evian	Red Dog
Service	delivery	to car	you bag it	delivery
Network	CBS	CNN	MSNBC	Fox

(We admit to broad generalizations. Not everyone fits neatly into a category defined by age or generation.)

Ask them! Using the above chart, imagine that a mature, a boomer, an Xer, and a Yer are in your office. How do you suppose each would answer if asked to:

- Clean the restrooms?
- Work overtime without notice?
- Name a hero?
- Assist a disabled person?
- Count change?
- Work nights or weekends?
- Perform a repetitive task for eight hours?
- Handle a difficult customer?
- Work for minimum wage?
- Read instructions?

The worker and the work have changed. Old ways just aren't going to work. The good news is we know what *will* work. So read on. Help is on the way!

7

POS AND SERVICE NATURALS

Maybe you've heard of it, this thing called Positively Outrageous Service. When we first introduced the idea of Positively Outrageous Service, we weren't so much inventing something as we were giving a name to a way of thinking about serving customers, both traditional and internal. We refer to it as POS. It has a long definition, but the short version is simply making customers say *wow!*

Three incredible things happen when a customer is wowed. First, a service wow creates a halo effect that leads the customer to believe that subsequent service experiences may be better than they really are. We don't know for sure how long a halo will persist or exactly how resistant a halo will be to service flaws. We only know that it's there and it matters.

Second, a service wow creates a tendency to reciprocate. As a customer, you feel psychologically compelled to do something in return. And result number three? Compelling, positive word of mouth.

HALO

A halo effect works both ways. If you expect poor service, it seems that the world unfolds for no reason other than to prove you right. If you expect great service, you aren't likely to be disappointed. No matter the quality of service you provide, your customers base their present service experience at least in part on their previous experience.

When I needed a slight adjustment to the sciatic nerve in my thigh, Buns bundled me up and hauled me off to a chiropractor who had a shiny new office with a well-trained staff. Unfortunately, the staff was more interested in my wallet than my back, scheduling me for a two-hour appointment for what turned out to be only a 10-minute adjustment. I was furious and informed the doctor-with-a-sales-pitch that the next visit would have to feature a lot less waiting.

On visit number two, I waited nearly 30 minutes before deciding I had other things to do. On visit number three (okay, I admit there shouldn't have been a visit number three, and I will tell you there wasn't a number four!), I was kept waiting! It was for a lot less time than I expected, but I nonetheless felt dumped on . . . again. Halo effect.

Across the county we found Dr. Andrea Wright. She is terrific! On our last visit she walked into the waiting room, touched Buns gently on the shoulder with a "Hello, nice to see you again," and struck up a brief conversation before taking me into the work area.

How long does Dr. Wright make me wait? I haven't a clue! Her office demeanor and attentiveness to my physical complaints have wrapped a halo effect around my visits. She's a goddess!

RECIPROCITY

It was a simple tin of cookies. Yes, they had been homemade the day before, and, yes, they are knock-out delicious. Still, they were just cookies; not the sort of thing that you would use to negotiate a deal on a rental car at Hertz or National.

There we were, standing on the tarmac in Palm Springs and watching the crew at Million Air chock the plane and hustle our bags onto an electric cart. We had met the good folks at Million Air Palm Springs a month earlier, mentioned that we would be in town for a speaking engagement, and weren't surprised to be invited to sample their version of customer service. So when the time came to pack, I fired up the computer to plan our flight, and Buns, in her inimitable style, fired up the oven to whip up a batch of goodness.

Now, we didn't expect to schmooze our way to a deal, but the folks on the ramp popped open the tin to inhale the smell of oatmeal scotchies, and they worked their magic. Five minutes later we were on our way in a car provided free, gratis, por nada.

A little something that gets you a big something. Sometimes unexpected. Reciprocity.

WORD OF MOUTH

The last and possibly the best benefit of Positively Outrageous Service is positive, compelling word of mouth. Word of mouth beats any kind of institutional marketing you can name. One happy customer suggesting to a potential customer that he or she gives you a try is, in the words of the Greek god Visa, priceless.

Positively Outrageous Service is the service story you can't wait to tell. It is the antithesis of the worst story you've ever had. Take a look at the definition of POS: It's random and unexpected; it's out of proportion to the circumstance; the customer is personally involved; and it creates positive, compelling word of mouth.

If that's the definition of the best customer service, how would you define the worst? It's the same definition! Substitute negative for positive, and you've got yourself a concept. Positively Outrageous Service gets customers talking about you in a positive way.

Salad Service

Sarah, a new customer service representative (CSR) with Business Aviation in Sioux Falls, was working the desk when the pilot of a corporate jet called to say he would be on the ramp in just over an hour. His passenger, a top CEO, was hungry for a cobb salad. "No problem," was the response. No problem except that Sarah had no idea what a cobb salad was. So she hopped on the Internet, found a recipe for a cobb salad, called a nearby restaurant, and placed the order. (Good thing she had the recipe as they had no idea what a cobb salad was either!)

To put the icing on the cake, Sarah asked for the salad to be delivered in a glass bowl rather than the usual Styrofoam container. If you are going to do it right, you might as well go all the way! And I'll bet in addition to being the most memorable salad, it was also one of the most expensive!

Only the Competent Qualify

There's no time for a setup. Check out these next three stories from service leader Southwest Airlines, and then we'll share an important point:

> I have always told myself that if I were going to get married, I would ask the question in a way that everyone would remember. So I decided to ask my girlfriend to marry me over the intercom on our flight. I said, "Attention, passengers, could I have Lillian M. report to the front of the plane?" I then got on one knee and popped the question and she answered "Yes!" The captain congratulated us over the intercom and on arrival the flight attendants sang "Going to the Chapel." I couldn't believe this was actually happening. How many other airlines could you see doing this?

> It seems we always come back to SWA! My daughter and I were taking a trip . . . and there were quite a few young children on the flight. As usual, the crew was wonderful, helping to get all the kids seated and comfortable. The flight was pretty uneventful until the last 15 minutes, when we ran into heavy turbulence. It was obvious that some of the little ones were getting scared.
>
> Over the loudspeaker came the captain's voice. "Well now, how'd you like that one? That one was for the kids! Almost better than Disneyland, right?" and every time the plane would drop or bump hard he would say, "Wee! Wasn't that one great? Wanna do it again?"
>
> Needless to say, the kids were delighted, and what might have been a fearful experience turned into fun. By the time we landed, most of the kids were smiling and laughing and thanking the captain for the great ride *and* he was shaking their hands as they left the plane!

> The flight attendants were great. They made a long, boring flight memorable, especially when they found out we were newlyweds. As they congratulated us, they passed out paper and pencils to the passengers and asked them to give us (the newlyweds) advice, suggestions, and recipes. Then, to top it off, they gave us a bottle of champagne when we landed.

Here's a big point, a huge point: Only competent organizations practice Positively Outrageous Service. Imagine turning a handful of young flight attendants loose on a $35 million aircraft at 35,000 feet above sea level doing .78 mach with 120 passengers on board and telling them to "Go play."

It takes an incredibly competent, and therefore confident, organization to do that. The rest are so afraid that someone will break a rule or abuse a policy. The result? "Put your seat back and tray table in its full upright and locked position. Do not move for the next three hours. This is a recording."

> **T**h i n k i n g   **P**o i n t
>
> *How could your team deliver Positively Outrageous Service?*

SERVICE NATURALS:
A PSYCHOLOGICAL PORTRAIT

Something wasn't right. Eerie tones were calling from the emergency services scanner on the table near my chair. They were also coming from the pager on my belt. Roused from a half-sleep, the kind you get from couches and too-comfortable chairs, I couldn't quite figure what was happening.

The tones that had caught me nodding over a huge pile of research were for me. My other life was calling, about to launch Buns and me into the night on a volunteer emergency medical service (EMS) run.

"Medic 2, Zone 2, first responders" was all it took to send me to the door.

"Sixty-seven-year-old unconscious male, not breathing." It was the last part of the phrase that made my heart race. The address was 6 miles away. Medic 2 was coming from nearly 12 miles. I would be first and almost certainly too late if this turned out to be what I suspected—a full cardiac arrest.

Pumping nearly 90 in the Toyota, I held out first the right hand followed by the left so Buns could install a pair of latex exam gloves and add her usual pat of reassurance. "You can beat him!" said Buns, offering driving assistance at the intersection, watching from her shotgun seat. In short order I was kneeling in the gravel beside a man who looked like death. (If you haven't seen Death, he is blue when he attends a full arrest.) Two bystanders were administering CPR (cardiopulmonary resuscitation), expertly coached by a voice from dispatch brought to the scene by cell phone.

I took over and applied my training. I inserted an airway adjunct, added a bag valve mask to pump O₂ (oxygen), attached the AED (automated external defibulator) in place, and then listened as its dispassionate synthesized voice said, "No shock advised. Continue CPR." When Medic 2 arrived, I yelled to the first medic off the box (EMS term for ambulance), "Airway kit! Airway!" And then the battle continued in earnest.

We were soon packaged and loaded, and the box waved past waiting traffic by the two sheriff's office deputies. Intubation had gone perfectly, one smooth move aided by a bit of cricoid pressure. The stick caught the vein on the first attempt. Even in death there was a moment to notice the beauty of a well-executed protocol. Now, at 70 miles an hour, treatment continued with my hanging on with one hand and attempting chest compressions with the other.

"I can't thank you enough for being here tonight," said the medic. He was pushing Epinephrine and then Lidocaine, administering shocks, and calling the Emergency Department. He was, to say the least, one busy guy. "My pleasure," I grunted, as we lurched around the bend by the local cemetery. "No, I mean I really thank you. This is my first full arrest as a paramedic. We were wondering on the way to the scene if you might be home, and I was glad when dispatch let us know you were on the way."

When the box slowed and started to back up, I could see the nurses in scrubs craning to see what we had brought to their doorstep. And soon it was over. The box sat empty, doors wide open, overhead work light glaring, and the floor littered with the debris of life's struggle. Alone I shopped its cabinets and crannies to replace my spent gear: a bag valve mask, a suction device, a nonrebreather mask, and a pair of bandage shears that no doubt had fallen from my bag.

"Scott!" I turned to face the crew, mere silhouettes in the dark. "Hey, thanks again for coming out tonight," as we shook hands. "Yeah, no problem. Sorry we lost. It was a good try." The lot may have been dark, but I caught, in the light spilling through the ER doors, one small tear from a pro who had given his best . . . and cared.

Service Naturals are everywhere. From paramedics who ply their trade in the back of racing ambulances to barmaids willing to linger just a little longer to hear a tale of loneliness, Service Naturals are everywhere. In this chapter we show you how to know one when you see one. For now, know that if you find a paramedic who hasn't lost the capacity to cry, you've found a Service Natural. They're special.

Holiday Inn Ruby

What is it that makes you remember a server for more than three decades? It must be something special.

When we moved to California, our first home was the Holiday Inn in Santa Monica. Mom, Dad, and the five boys would troop down to the coffee shop, order breakfast, and start another day in wonderment over all the things that we noticed were different from what we no longer called home. The flowering bushes along the freeway, the surprise that the San Fernando Valley wasn't green like the valleys of Kentucky . . . and then, of course, the lady shopping in a bikini were all very different.

One thing that did feel like home was a red-headed waitress named Ruby. Within a couple of days, she was calling us by name and remembering that I liked my eggs sunny-side up. Was she a great waitress? Maybe not in the traditional sense, but remember, service is defined by the customer.

"Miss Ruby?" (We were from the South.) "May I have another glass of orange juice?" And Miss Ruby would glide by our table, slowing just enough to pinch my cheek and saying, "Oh, you're so cute!" And while I sat and waited and waited and waited, the wait never seemed too long because I was holding the thought, "Hey, maybe I *am* cute!"

Miss Ruby was a *Service Natural,* a term that has little to do with technical ability and everything to do with the ability to relate on a human level.

Palace Café

Sometimes when we fly our little plane along the Gulf Coast, we look out the window in search of an excuse to stop. In the summertime our excuse is often thunderstorms. Once in a while it's the Palace Café in New Orleans.

If you want great service, any table will do but we choose to look for a table commanded by Jim McDaniel. Now, how do you suppose I remember the name of a server in a restaurant that we visit only a couple of times a year? It's simple. He gave us his card. Yep! A server with a business card. Now, that guy is a Service Natural!

"I became really good at adapting my style to the different personalities of my customers. The best salespeople see things through their customers' eyes, modify their styles to their customers' chemistry, and pull together their offering to meet their customers' needs. But being in front of the customer doesn't help if you do all the talking." (Beth Klein, President and CEO, GE Medical Systems)

Let's Go Flying!

The wrinkled boarding pass says it was American Airlines flight 2451 from San Antonio to San Jose with an intermediate stop in Dallas. My scribbled note on the back says the captain was Jim Hummel. Here's how I remember it.

When I first heard the voice, I guessed it was the captain, but I was buried so far in the back of the plane there was no point in looking up. Had I been in first class, I would have glanced toward the cockpit door. (We were still at the gate and the door would be open.) But I did look up, drawn by the words and the tone to see a fit-looking pilot standing in the cabin, using the PA system normally reserved for bored flight attendants.

"Good morning, folks. I'm Captain Jim Hummel, and I'd like to share a few thoughts with you while we are waiting for the last few bags to be loaded. Actually, I have two thoughts. First, I'd like to welcome aboard the fine men and women from our armed services. I want to tell them how much we appreciate them and all they do for this great country." (This was shortly after the fall of Afghanistan to coalition forces.)

The cabin was filled with applause, and I had the distinct feeling that the passengers wished they had applauded even louder, but they had been caught by surprise by the captain's unusual preflight announcement. "I also want to thank each of you for flying with us today. Not only is this important to American Airlines but it is important to our entire nation. So I thought I would take just a moment to express our heartfelt thanks. God bless you and God bless America. Now, let's go flying."

That, ladies and germs, is a Service Natural. What is it that draws a busy captain from the duties of the cockpit to make an announcement that could just as easily have gone unmade? How is it that a server will pinch the cheek of a young boy and cause him to blush in embarrassment? There is only one explanation. Great servers are just . . . different. Are they trained to be different? Maybe. Are they born to be different? Definitely.

We were surprised on one extremely hot day to see a well-known contractor doff his shirt and attack a landscaping problem with a shovel. I asked him why he didn't wait for his crew and equipment. Without looking up, the contractor recited a simple mantra. I could imagine his long-deceased daddy smiling from above as he said, "Get off your butt and onto your feet . . . get out of the shade and into the heat! Poor people have poor ways."

And for your listening entertainment, read on:

"Ladies and Gentlemen, we'll be landing at Gate 31. The gate agent meeting the flight will have connecting information. But we'll make it easy; your gate is in another terminal. If this is your final destination, there is no need to worry about your baggage. It's not on this flight."

"Welcome aboard flight 1313. We'd like to give special recognition to our copilot, who just completed flight school, for his persistence . . . and to the school for letting him repeat the course twice. Our pilot today is Captain Lucky, back on the job after his second heart attack."

(These come from flying Southwest during its early days, when it had only one rented plane.)

EVERY EMPLOYEE IS PERFECT!

Thinking back on some of the screwball employees I've hired—and fired—it seems almost like lying to say this but it's true: Everyone has the potential to be a great employee . . . somewhere.

I remember the fry cook at Denny's who had the unsettling habit of throwing a chef knife across the kitchen anytime he was upset. And he was always upset!

I remember the car salesman who sold a struggling young couple a two-seater sports car, even though the wife was eight months pregnant. Obviously, there was a bonus for selling that particular vehicle. It didn't matter that it was a piece of junk and totally inappropriate for the customers.

And then there was the sales executive who spent the day on the golf course and called it networking. He could have been a good salesperson, just not in an unstructured environment.

Still, I stand by my statement. Everyone has the potential to be a great employee . . . somewhere.

Another somewhere. Employees who aren't living up to their potential won't often be helped by training. Employees who aren't performing may just need another somewhere to be!

The reason service stinks is not so much a matter of stinky servers as it is a matter of the right people in the wrong place. We mistakenly put people in jobs where they are being asked for performance that their psychological makeup prohibits!

Sure, for a while the dating personality (you'll learn more about this later) will rear its smiling head and almost anyone can remember to say, "Have a nice day." But saying it and meaning it are two different things; and eventually "Have a nice day" gets said through clenched teeth.

> **T** *h i n k i n g* **P** *o i n t*
>
> *Poor customer service is more a matter of miscasting than inadequate training.*

Where is somewhere? If there is a right job for everyone, where is it? How do we know where everyone fits?

There *is* a right job for everyone. To know where everyone fits, we must first define the "somewheres."

> **T** *h i n k i n g* **P** *o i n t*
>
> *To hire accurately, you must first define the job requirements in behavioral terms.*

TEN PLUS CHARACTERISTICS OF A CUSTOMER SERVICE PRO

It's natural that a book on customer service would have a list of ten characteristics of a Service Natural. But that's not possible for two reasons. First, great customer service is always defined by the needs of the customer at any particular moment; and, second, I came up with more than ten!

1. Greets customers without delay
2. Offers a friendly greeting
3. Recognizes each customer as an individual
4. Offers help where appropriate
5. Has a no-pressure sales approach
6. Spends time freely (explaining, conversation)
7. Devotes full attention to transaction
8. Asks questions to determine needs (in a nonpressure way)

9. Physically demonstrates product where appropriate
10. Is willing and able to answer questions
11. Is able to locate products quickly
12. Has a professional appearance and language
13. Speaks well of company and product
14. Handles product with respect
15. Looks for opportunities to serve
16. Does not offer a canned presentation
17. Suggests solutions tailored to each customer

Great customer service is defined by the customer. Imagine how an engineer working on a problem might define great customer service: "I just want to hear the facts." Now, how about a bar patron who is working on a problem? "Let me tell you the facts." And there's always the possibility of an engineer sitting at a bar working on a problem: "She left me. What is the probability of that happening on a date ending in three?"

T *h i n k i n g* **P** *o i n t*

How would your various customers define great customer service?

FAULTY FIT

The biggest cause of stinky customer service is a mismatch between the behavioral requirements of the job and the personality of the applicant or incumbent. Bill Wagner of ACCORD Management Systems likes to point out that the first-time divorce rate is more than 50 percent, yet we can't imagine anyone believing that his or her marriage will end in divorce. If that is the case, then ponder the following major thought: If you can't figure out whom you're marrying after three years of dating, then how in tarnation can you figure out whom you're hiring after only a 30-minute interview? It's almost impossible to know.

To get the right player on the right team, you have to know what constitutes the requirements of the position and the makeup of the right player. Do this by benchmarking or profiling top performers and hiring more just like them! If you keep hiring the same way you've always been hiring, you'll get more of what you always have. If you're happy with that, fine! But remember that old definition for the word *insanity?* Insanity is doing the same thing but expecting a different result.

If you're not happy with the customer service at your place, keep this thought in mind.

> **T** h i n k i n g   **P** o i n t
>
> *The team you've got isn't going to take you where you want to go because if they were capable of doing that, you'd already be there!*

What is the next step? *Strengthen recruiting.* The big players in the service game have it made; they have marketing departments. Unfortunately, not many recognize that recruiting is a marketing problem; if they did, few would want the responsibility. It isn't glamorous. It isn't sexy. But great recruiting and hiring will sell a potload of product. Simply stated, treat recruiting like the marketing problem that it is.

Here are several more fit-curing steps: (1) Be more selective. (2) Hire slowly. (3) Fire fast.

The first responsibility is to the organization, not the individual. Enron was all about looking out for number one (and two and three and four but not number 20,863.) If someone, even yourself, is not good for the long-term viability of the corporate body, that person's got to go and sooner rather than later.

Every time I've fired a nonperformer, it was too late but generated a huge sigh of relief from the employees who had been carrying the nonperformer's weight.

> **T** h i n k i n g   **P** o i n t
>
> *How do your customers define great service?*
>
> **T** h i n k i n g   **P** o i n t
>
> *How could you use marketing techniques to strengthen recruiting?*
>
> **T** h i n k i n g   **P** o i n t
>
> *Who on your team needs to work somewhere else?*

Part Two

PERSONALITY THEMING

The Research and Methodology

8

NATURE OR NURTURE?

I'm the oldest. Steve is next, followed by Stuart and Stacy. All those S names confused my dad to the point that he just called all of us Sam. Line us up and you probably wouldn't think we had any shared genetics. Spend a few minutes talking to us (and other than a shared gift of gab), you'd be certain we were each adopted: one from the circus, one found on the doorstep of the library, and the other two straight from the children's home.

How do you account for the behavior that is who we are? Is it genetic? Is it how we are nurtured? It's a little bit of both. However you slice it, "I yam what I yam what I yam." And if you hire the wrong people in the first place, the best you can hope for is they will leave on their own, and soon!

Nature provides us with certain innate abilities, such as a predilection to math or a physique designed to sprint rather than run marathons, but it is nurture that turns these raw materials into the behaviors that make us, us! Let's not argue over whether slothful people are born or raised. Let's give poor performers the benefit of a liberal doubt and blame unproductive behavior completely on the sins of an uncaring society. We are still left with the fact that even the best corporate training program is unlikely to override years of poor habits.

HIRE FOR ATTITUDE—TRAIN FOR SKILLS

For the same reason that marrying with the idea that you are going to change those few annoying habits that make you nuts, hiring someone who isn't a fit right from the get-go is going to end in divorce. Spare yourself, spare the candidate, and, for goodness sake, spare your customers and your bottom line. Be relentless (perhaps ruthless) when it comes to hiring "juuuust" right.

Mysterious Thirds

By the end of this chapter and certainly by the end of the book, I promise you will be sold on the value of *profiling*. After you have instituted a properly designed program in your organization, you will never go back to hiring based on gut instinct and the usual cursory reference check.

What you may not have considered is that what goes for hiring goes double for promoting. When I worked for a large quick-service restaurant chain, I managed to convince the folks at the head shed to invest in a simple prehire profile system. The results were astounding. We had wanted to build a profile solely for our company and were particularly concerned if it would be seen as valid with the EEOC. No one wanted to defend a charge of adverse impact.

We took our list of over 1,000 restaurant managers and divided them into three groups. Highest sales and profit managers were in one group, lowest in yet another group, and all the rest assigned to the remaining group. We profiled the top and bottom groups knowing that if no significant difference between the two appeared, there would be no reason for continuing. Well, they were different, hugely different.

As an aside, let me say that any profile question has the potential to be valid or not, depending on whether it actually discriminates (legally, of course.) Whatever area you explore, you must validate first!

In short order, we had customized our profiling instrument and were confident that it would be an accurate predictor of performance. Initially, a chorus of moans and groans arose from operations. They complained about having to spend a few bucks to purchase an instrument for each potential candidate. We made things a little better when we told them that it was unnecessary to profile everyone; save the expense for those who make it past the first impression and initial interview.

The next problem came when the field guys started to complain that the profiles were knocking out what had otherwise seemed to be excellent candidates. "The profile doesn't work," they complained. Their efforts at recruiting were said to have doubled. "This thing stinks," was the general consensus. Then something happened. First, word came from the one division that had adopted the program hook, line, and sinker. At its regional training school, participants noticed a sudden decrease in attrition. It seemed—and the numbers soon backed it up—that almost every candidate hired by using the new profile was graduating from the school.

In short order, reports from the other schools began to trickle in, telling of similar results. The corporate trainers wanted to claim a spontaneous improvement in teaching, but we all knew—it was the profile. Better candidates led to lower attrition, which soon translated into the need to hire fewer but harder.

So we got bold and pitched using a profile in making promotion decisions. The logical place to begin was the next job level above store manager. This job position, area manager who supervised six to ten units, typically covered a compact geographical territory that was usually, but not always, in a metropolitan area. Logically, the best store managers would make the best area managers. Logically.

To save money on a validation survey, top management asked me to use the same profile we had developed for hiring store managers, and logically that seemed to make sense. Because our experience with profiling was relatively new, all of our long-time, successful store managers, who were most likely ready for promotion, had been hired well before our profiling had begun.

"Just run these folks through the profile and tell us which ones we should consider," was the directive from the top. We suspected that might not work, and we weren't certain about an adverse impact, so we whined for approval of a limited test. And boy, were we surprised!

We began by profiling the existing area managers, breaking that smaller group into thirds just as we had done with the store manager position. We created a composite profile of each third and again discovered a gaping difference between our most successful group and the others.

The surprise came when we discovered that our most successful store managers did not promote well. It turned out that the behaviors necessary to run a single unit were not nearly the same as those required to supervise an area! In fact, it turned out that managers from the middle group of store performers actually made better area supervisors than did the top-performing single unit group!

What if you were one of the top-performing single store managers? How would you feel? Probably cheated. On the other hand, you would be less subject to being promoted out of your comfort zone; you would be less likely to be promoted to a job you couldn't handle; and the company would be less likely to trade a great store manager for a mediocre multiunit supervisor. Or you would be promoted, and your boss would be charged with giving you the support your profile said you would need.

What did we learn? Several great points.

T h i n k i n g   P o i n t

Profiling toughens the hiring process but results in less hiring through lowered attrition.

T h i n k i n g   P o i n t

Profiles that are valid for one job may not be valid for a similar job, even though the jobs seem similar in nature.

T h i n k i n g   P o i n t

Profiles are as important in promotion decisions as they are in the hiring decision.

9

THE RESEARCH

"**I**t only costs a dollar more to go first class." That's what my Uncle Jed always said. Of course, he died poor, so maybe he wasn't really a reliable source! When we wanted a first-class partner for our research, we chose Bill Wagner and his crew at ACCORD Management Systems in Westlake Village, California. (You can peek at what they do at accordsyst.com) The ACCORD folks are behavioral gurus and represent The McQuaig System™ as their tool of choice.

ACCORD came to us with the experience, the tools, the right questions, and a huge body of research that we also tap, but we started this project with a slightly different bent. It seems that half the world has been studying salespeople and that's fine except in this economy there are more service persons than salespersons. We wanted to discover what it is that makes a great service person, a Service Natural. We also wanted to know how leadership and customership might influence the expression of customer service. So in addition to the data from ACCORD, we decided to fish in different waters. We wanted to define in no uncertain terms what a Service Natural is. We also wanted to be able to know one when we saw one or, in ACCORD's case, measured one.

Intuitively we know that Service Naturals must possess some of the following traits: They must inspire trust; they must believe serving others is a reward in itself; they must be good communicators; they must have lots of energy; and they must be very perceptive and empathetic. That's the intuitive definition. What we wanted to know was how Service Naturals might be defined by their customers and by the people who hire and manage them. To find out, we asked a number of our clients to participate in a four-part research project.

Part one asked the leader of the participating organization's service effort to define in his or her terms what constituted a great service person. We wanted to know if executives are actually looking for the right person when they recruit.

In part two we asked participating organizations to identify their top customer service providers and complete the McQuaig Job Survey.® Because this behavioral tool measures the behavioral requirements of any position, we didn't define for them what a great customer service person is. We let them decide, using any standards they chose. Most organizations that participated simply selected service persons about which customers said good things. This is both a strength and a consideration of our research.

Great customer service is defined *by the customer* and because customers' desires vary from industry to industry (even moment to moment), we intentionally left the definition of great customer servers up to the research participants.

The strength of that approach is producing profiles that are industry-specific. The built-in downside is that our composite profile of a Service Natural will be only generally right. But the surprise was that even our "generally right" profile is miles apart from what managers, specifically good managers, hold to be common knowledge!

To carry this thought to its logical conclusion, imagine two Service Naturals working for the same company, one working in Peoria and the other in Dallas. The behavioral personality requirements of these two cities may be different because their markets are so different. Just because it plays in Peoria doesn't mean that it plays in Dallas.

Part three of our research will drive liberals nuts: We surveyed *service losers*. (Sorry, I couldn't resist the term. But trust me, we never once used the term in practice, and I only use it now because it reflects general, although completely erroneous, thinking.) There are no absolute service losers, although as a customer you might think differently. But there are service folks who are so miserably miscast that even they don't think much of themselves!

The terminology we used with our research partners was a profile of service folks defined as "struggling." We had to do this to defend our definition of Service Naturals. Without also identifying service strugglers, we would have had no way of differentiating between the two groups.

A final piece of research completed our study. We asked 10,000 customers to share their feelings about service and tell us their tactics for actually getting the service they want. (More about this later.)

Into the Pool

Every personality is the right personality for something. But a personality perfect for one position might be disastrous in another. We did not set out to discover a single, perfect customer service personality for any and every service situation. We set out to discover the perfect personalities (plural) for a variety of situations.

Fortunately, our clients are as kind as they are diverse, so it took no more than a few afternoons on the telephone to cobble together a band of volunteer guinea pigs. We wanted a wide variety of industries represented and we got them!

Even though we have said that no single personality profile is best for every service occasion, we were curious to see if there might at least be similarities. And there are . . . sorta. In our research survey we have bankers, auto dealers, and credit unions in addition to fast-food, not-so-fast food, and convenience store operators along with retail clothiers and airplane service providers. We pretty much have the bases covered.

It won't be hard for you to find a profile study that comes close to reflecting your industry. But be careful. Even the smallest differences could make huge changes in the personality requirements that create a perfect fit for you and your customers. And we realize that it's even too broad to say that we have a recommended best personality for an industry because many job positions are in any one industry. A number of rules, however, make this process both practical and predictable.

For example, we surveyed auto dealers to discover a best personality fit for a service writer—that is, the man or woman who checks in your car and carefully listens as you describe the screech-grind noise you hear from the transmission every time you shift from drive to reverse without coming to a complete stop. The personality of the perfect service writer isn't anywhere near the personality required to sell you the vehicle nor the required personality for the technician who will repair your vehicle.

And that brings us to an important point: Profiling a personality, as we noted previously, is just as valuable when considering an employee for promotion as it is when you're making the initial hire. Actually, it may be more important because you are risking the career of a proven performer. In the behavioral world we refer to this as a Peter Principle promotion.

Take our automobile service writers for example. Where do you think most service writers worked before being promoted to their present position? You guessed it; they were service technicians (mechanics). And wouldn't you know the personality required to be a highly successful technician is much different from that required to meet and greet customers! Technicians work with stuff, and service writers work with people. (We'll see more on this later!)

The Profile

The McQuaig Word Survey® uses what is known as the *forced response* approach to determine your personality relative to four pairs of contrasting personality dimensions. Dominant is paired with accepting. Sociability pairs nicely with analytical. Relaxation matches against driving and compliance is balanced opposite independence. A series of skillfully crafted forced choices lead to a score that determines the plot of your graph.

For the sake of simplicity, I'll be using a different, but similar, graph (shown in Figure 9.1).

Notice that the midpoint is labeled average. The higher or lower the graph goes, so does the intensity of the behavioral factor. I describe the changes as "average," "tends to," "is," "very," and "extremely." Additional adjectives help to describe the intensity of each factor. Personalities don't jump from average to extreme; instead, our temperaments fall at many points along a continuum. For example, somewhere between average and extremely dominant, you might find "self-starter," then "assertive," followed by "aggressive." In between average sociability and sociable lie "warm," followed by "extroverted" and then "extremely persuasive." For our purposes, remember that personality isn't a matter of all or none.

Before I close the discussion, I'll provide you with enough understanding to approximate the benefits of a written or online profile in a traditional interviewing session. Just remember I said "approximate." The best course would be to use these new techniques and understandings to supercharge your interviewing skills and then use a true profiling instrument to verify your choice.

FIGURE 9.1 *Graph Format*

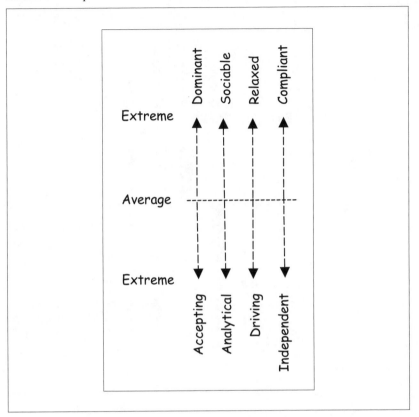

The Dating Personality

To begin the project we profiled our small business family and surprise . . . we're not all perfect fits! So how do you explain the fact that we work so well together and, I think, do a great job? Here's the discovery: Almost any personality can be put on hold long enough to accomplish a short-term goal.

Bill Wagner has referred to the following as what he calls "the dating personality," which looks something like the graph in Figure 9.2.

Dating is selling. "Look at me. I'm lovable.You're lovable, too!"

The dating personality is accepting. "Cats? I love cats! And isn't it cute how they poop in that little box in the living room!"

The dating personality is sociable. "I love walks on the beach at sunset. Oh, my day job? I'm an engineer."

FIGURE 9.2   *The Dating Personality*

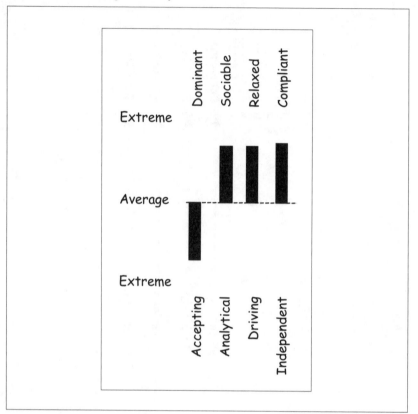

The dating personality is relaxed. "It doesn't matter that we're late. There's always another movie."

And the dating personality is compliant. "What do you want to do?" "I don't know. Whatever you want to do."

The point is this: While we are dating (and interviewing), most of us are quite capable of projecting a personality that is completely different from our everyday or true personality.

A con man or even a good public speaker might be a great example of someone's adopting a style for a short period of time. My profile (speaker, not con artist) reveals the unvarnished truth: In person, I'm shy, a natural-born wallflower. I'm just not what you would call a social butterfly. The good news is that I *am* capable of entertaining an audience . . . as in keeping them in stitches . . . for at least as long as it takes to deliver a keynote.

FIGURE 9.3 *Scott's Natural Behavior*

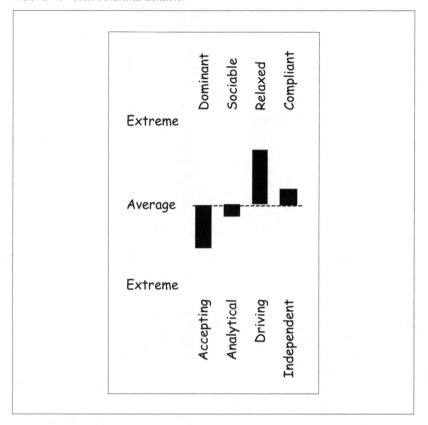

My real personality looks like the graph in Figure 9.3: very accepting, tending toward egg-headed, very relaxed and casual, and compliant. This is the picture of a guy who is happy being alone with his nose stuck in a book, one who will pretty much go along to get along.

Now, slide in the graph in Figure 9.4 of my attempted personality, the guy I am for short bursts. What you see on this graph is a fellow who is the life of the party, very focused, uninhibited, and strong-willed. That's me at work, an entirely different person from my private self.

Is this good or bad? It depends on the level of performance. Personalities are neither good nor bad. It depends on what you want the personality to do. The only thing that matters is having the right personality for the job or the right job for the personality.

The greater the difference between the real self and the attempted self, the more difficult it is to sustain the attempted personality. Exhibiting an attempted personality that is much different from the real personality creates stress and requires energy.

FIGURE 9.4 *Scott's Attempted Behavior*

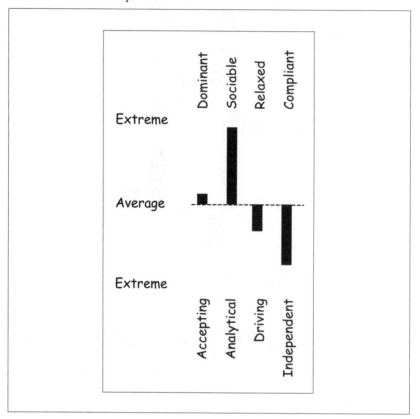

The Talmud, a religious book of 613 laws, rules, and regulations, says that prior to marriage, a woman should see her intended under three circumstances: when he is drunk, when he is sick, and when he is angry. Why do you suppose this is so? Because these are the times when we are under stress, that we are most likely to reveal our real selves.

Take another look at Figure 9.3 and tell me if this is the graph of a macho man. (Pssst! It's not!) I am hardly what you would consider a man's man. I don't drink. I don't smoke. I don't chase women (well, one). I don't even scratch inappropriately! Mr. Accepting, Relaxed, and Compliant isn't the kind of guy to cause a scene—or is he? Keep reading and I'll show you that we are not limited to a single attempted style.

Personality, it turns out, is purely situational. The challenge for the boss is to predict which personality will show up for the interview and which will ultimately show up for work.

Stand Up!

We were in St. Louis at the Adams Mark Hotel, where the chairman and founder of a large organization was scheduled to speak, to be followed by a short break and my address as the official opener of the conference of 300 general managers plus corporate staff. I found a seat near the door in the back, the last row, where someone familiar with the profile of my real personality would expect me to sit.

I sat there—fat, dumb, happy, and paying no particular attention—until Mr. Chairman said these words, "I am tired of our great President Bill Clinton being trashed for what is no more than a minor sexual indiscretion. We've all done things we shouldn't have done, but that's no excuse for the way they are treating our president. Anyone who has never had a minor sexual indiscretion, stand up." No one stood. They were shocked.

Later, Mr. Chairman said, "I asked earlier and probably surprised you. So now, here's another chance. If you have never had a minor sexual indiscretion, stand up." No one did.

At the break I raced to tell Buns, who was reading in the lobby. She was furious. "Did you stand up?" (Isn't it like a wife to want to know?)

"Well, no. I was sitting in the back minding my own business, and I didn't want to be the only one to stand and have him ask who I was."

Then it was my turn to speak . . . I made it about halfway, and then something in my material gave me an ideal opening. "Earlier we were asked to stand up, and I am embarrassed to tell you that I did not. I felt that as your speaker I didn't want to get involved with a private matter. But I want you to know I am standing up now."

Crowd goes wild!

Stay with me. A point is about to be made!

Deep Pockets

"Your lip is bleeding." I licked and tasted blood and, even though I realized it had been of my own doing, I was just a little angry. It's a quirk, one of those oddball habits. We all have them and one of mine is biting my lip when under stress. I never notice it when I'm doing it. Only afterwards and this was afterwards.

Mario, Brenda, Buns, and I were in Paris. Four middle-aged businesspeople off to see the world in search of adventure. An hour earlier we had come close to more than we bargained for. About 5:30 PM we had boarded the subway at Place de Clichy on the western edge of the

Montmartre district, a few stops from our hotel. I'm fascinated by trains to the point that Buns sometimes reaches over and pushes up my lower jaw to stop my obvious gawking. Today was no exception. When the engine whooshed by and then screeched to a stop to present an open car door in front of us, I was playing my usual small-town-kid-visits-the-big-city self.

Mario was first; and then Brenda, Buns, and I entered. Somehow, a tall man in his mid-30s pushed his way ahead of the two women and took up a position at the center post, leaving just enough room for me to board but not so much as an extra inch. I was facing the center of the car.

As the doors began to close, one or maybe two other passengers shoved their way onto the train with the usual, expected bumping and then a little more bumping that struck me as neither usual nor expected. Instinctively, I felt for my wallet, and it was gone! My wallet had been in the front left pocket of my hiking shorts in a small pocket with a Velcro closure, somewhere safe. Somewhere it could not fall out. Somewhere that I would feel if not hear it should the flap be opened.

To my left was a 30ish man with a hawk nose and penetrating eyes. He was facing the door, wearing a polo shirt, and carrying his sport coat over his arm and hand. Polo shirt. Sport coat. Covering his hand. Something wasn't right. Behind him was an older, well-dressed man who faced me directly.

Several thoughts flashed through my mind. My wallet is missing, and it didn't fall out; I was bumped more than expected; here is a guy with his coat over his hand standing just inches away; and, finally, this train is going to stop in a matter of seconds. If my intuition is right, my wallet will be gone forever.

"What did you do?" I shouted at a face now trying harder than ever to ignore me. "I felt you bump me. Now empty your pockets!" I gripped his forearm to prevent any quick moves and then, because I wasn't sure about the older gentleman, who appeared to be my age, I invited him to the party, saying, "And if he doesn't come up with my wallet, you can plan on emptying your pockets, too!"

"Look! Look! I don't have it!" Hawk eyes moved slightly to reveal my wallet on the car floor. And there it was! Mario moved close and now held the culprit by the elbow. Funny that just hours ago we had remarked how good it was to have a friend you could count on to watch your back. I scooped up the wallet and quickly checked that my cards and ID were all there.

Out of the corner of my eye I noticed the other passengers looking on dumbstruck when Buns, in an effort to rally support from any possible Americans on board should I need it, said the most unusual thing. "He (the thief) doesn't know he's dealing with a kick-ass Texan!" Maybe she was just proud to see her husband, who looks like an accountant, taking charge of a tense situation. But later, back in our hotel room she would tell me that her right knee had been shaking a mile a minute. And then she said such magic words, "You're my hero."

Other thoughts poured through my mind. Should I call the police or take him to the police? Is he alone or is the big guy part of the routine? And what if he's armed? So I took the John Wayne approach and snarled, "Get off at the next stop or you're a dead man." And he did!

Information, intuition, and intention are what I believed saved my wallet and self respect.

The Unintentional Hero

It was an early West Coast morning, but I was awake and operating on Central Time. My flight was hours away, so I opted for breakfast at the beach and a chance to break out the camera that is always with me. Chances for a great shoot weren't good because it was pitch dark and spitting a cold rain. Still, I threw my bag into the rental car, pointed towards Venice Beach.

I was looking for an omelet but found trouble instead. Beneath a street light a huge man was struggling with a petite, pony-tailed woman. I slowed a bit and lowered the window on the passenger side to be sure I was seeing what I was seeing. "Damn!" was all I could think to say while finishing the thought mentally, "Damn! I wish I hadn't seen that. Now I have to do something."

Thinking had slowed my reactions just enough to allow the car to sail 20 or so feet downstream of the action. I pulled into the shadows, slammed the transmission into park, and stepped into the street. From an apartment window beyond the sidewalk and a low chain-link fence, a voice about as old as mine shouted, "Help her, dude! Help her! He's been beating on her for a long time!" As if it might do some good, I shouted, "Call the police and then (through clenched teeth for emphasis added) get out here!"

At close range the big man looked bigger: six-two or -three or even -four. A big guy with red hair, dressed like a mountaineer. I grabbed his wrist and said with all the intention in the world, two short words: "Let . . . go." And he did! To tell you the truth, we were both surprised!

Striking while the iron was hot, I pulled the girl to my car while mountain man stood with his mental pants around his knees. She dove into the passenger side as I jumped behind the wheel, locking her door as I did. Mountain man recovered and raced a few long strides to recover his prize. I found the window button just as he reached to unlock her door. As the window rose we drove off into the mist.

It turned out that the girl's assailant had just been released from prison and had surprised her by hiding in her apartment until she returned from work. His intention? To kidnap her and take her to live with him in the wilds of Oregon.

My intention? Do the right thing. So the story ends. My lip was bleeding. (Stress from exhibiting an attempted personality radically different from the real one!)

THE BIG FINISH

If all you knew about me was what you could learn from the above stories, would you want to hire me for a job in customer service? (Probably not, but the fit might be perfect for selling time-shares!)

Let's see how that personality—my attempted one—might profile as shown in Figure 9.5. No doubt, high dominance. There wouldn't be much sociability with perhaps a slight tendency toward the analytical. (Thinking on his feet, trying to decide the next move.) Driving might be expressed in a big way, and this personality is definitely independent.

Wouldn't it be nice to know if the personality you see in an interview is real or merely attempted? The better profiling systems on the market show both real and attempted personalities. The closer the fit between real and attempted, the less that stress figures into the equation.

ON THE FLY

Naturally, nothing quite beats a full profile instrument, but as Yogi Berra said, "You can see a lot by looking." You plan to meet a few new friends for dinner, and what do we know? First, that you are probably high in sociability. If you weren't, you wouldn't have made the date or you would have wanted to meet only one of them. One says to the server, "I'd like the fish, but I only want a half portion, please." Another says to the group, "Is anyone else not too hungry? We could share an entrée."

FIGURE 9.5 *Scott aka Rambo*

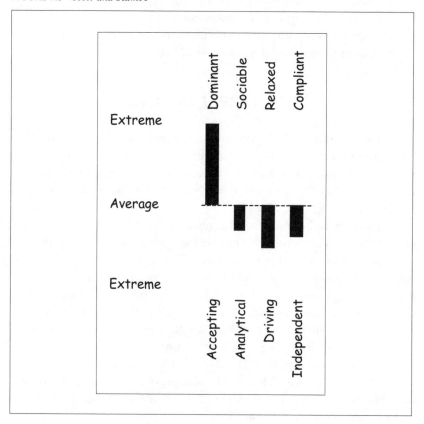

Another of the friends just says, "Okay," when the server tells her she can't give separate checks.

Who's in the group? You, the sociable one, along with a dominant, another sociable, and a compliant. See? Just pay attention!

A man walks into a bar, pulls up a stool, and in a loud voice says, "A round for everyone!" Another man walks into the bar and heads straight for a booth in a dark corner away from the action. Yet another man walks into the bar, carefully wipes his feet on the doormat, neatly hangs his hat and coat on the rack, sees a sign that says wait to be seated, and stands patiently at the door. A horse walks into the bar and the bartender says, "So why the long face?" (Sorry! I couldn't resist this!)

Here are a few other clues:

- Disruptive or demanding of attention: high dominant
- Interrupts frequently: high sociable
- Careful, thoughtful decision maker: high relaxed

- Caught up in details: high compliant
- Quiet and accepting: low dominant
- Appears to not be paying attention: low relaxed or driving
- Fails to follow directions: low compliant or independent

MISINTERPRETATIONS

A low sociable will be a poor communicator, but a high sociable will be a good conversationalist. Not necessarily! Communicating *easily* is not the same as communicating *effectively*. A low sociable's style may be matter-of-fact, strictly business, tending to be blunt but clear, whereas a high sociable might fail to listen.

Aggressive is domineering. Aggressive here means the drive to take charge and be goal focused. It's not necessarily the same as being pushy.

Low sociable folks don't get along with others. Nope, they just may take a while to warm up and will be more comfortable in smaller groups. If they are high dominant they may simply be blunt. Bill Wagner calls this his cricket theory of communication. Imagine a warm Texas evening with a yard full of crickets. What are they doing? They are chirping . . . because they feel safe in their environment, where they trust each other and are comfortable. What happens when you walk into the yard? They become quiet! Crickets are a lot like introverts. As long as they are in an environment where they feel safe, trust one another, and are comfortable, they communicate like extroverts.

Low dominant/high compliant folks find it challenging to be good managers. They may not be charismatic leaders, but in certain circumstances where their technical expertise is key, they are great resources for the team, even though they prefer to be off doing their own thing. They manage based on their level of expertise.

What You See versus What You Get

When it comes to personality, what you see may not be what you hire. For as long as we are dating (or interviewing), we can demonstrate a personality that is really quite appealing or, at the very least, appropriate!

Jim Collins, writing in *Good to Great* (Harper Collins, 2001), contends "It's who you pay, not how you pay them." The overriding factor in corporate greatness, says Collins, is the quality of the team. Using the analogy of a bus, he writes that in great companies "people either stayed on the bus for a long time or got off the bus in a hurry. In other words . . . they do not churn more, they churn better."

The lesson is simple: hire slow, fire fast. Unfortunately, most of us learned the lesson, in reverse—hire fast, fire slowly.

One lazy afternoon in Santa Barbara, I watched consultant Bill Wagner pepper a group of successful CEOs with questions about their hiring practices.

"Who has recently made a large purchase decision?"

A gentleman near the front nodded. (CEOs don't raise their hands; they just nod wisely.)

"What were you buying and how much did you spend?"

"A new computer system, close to a hundred thousand."

"And who has recently hired a top executive?" Wagner asked quickly to keep his questions close against the answers. Another head nodded, this time from the back of the room.

"What position were you filling?"

"A marketing director. It was just like Jim's purchase, about a hundred thousand."

"How much time did you invest as part of your due diligence in deciding which computer to buy?" A finger pointed to Jim.

"The better part of six months. All the choices seemed good and we didn't want to make a mistake. All in all, about 200 hours of research."

"And your marketing director? Was it six months? Six weeks? How many times did you interview your final selection?"

"Twice." The voice was sheepish, coming from a CEO.

"And how is he now doing?"

"He only lasted six months."

"I rest my case!"

Bill's point is simple: We agonize over an equipment purchase and gloss over key hiring decisions. Why is that? Equipment acquisition is largely an objective decision, whereas selecting or promoting an individual is more subjective. The key is to embrace a behavioral system so that the selection process becomes objective and predictable.

T h i n k i n g   **P** o i n t

What you see may *be what you get. Profile to be sure.*

T h i n k i n g   **P** o i n t

Hire slowly–fire quickly.

10

HOW TO HIRE PERFORMERS

Mickey Gilley might have had us in mind when he sang the song "Looking for Love." You remember the rest of the refrain . . . "in all the wrong places" . . . and that's precisely what we see with the results of our first research partner to complete its portion of the study.

We promised anonymity, so we won't tell you who the players are, but look at Figure 10.1. It depicts what management said would be the perfect customer service personality for *its* business. Take a look. These folks are looking for big, take-charge, highly independent, and sociable personalities.

Now check out Figure 10.2, on page 80, which is the composite of this partner's top customer service people. The difference in the desired personality and that of the actual top performers is astonishing!

The top performers for this particular business unit are surprisingly average. No, let's say they are balanced in each of the dimensions with just a slight tendency to thrive under pressure. We can reveal that the business in the survey is highly rules based and requires accuracy by the performers. Notice how the boss feels a strong dose of independence would be ideal, whereas the top performers say no, you have to err on the side of compliance.

FIGURE 10.1   *Boss's Ideal Customer Service Rep*

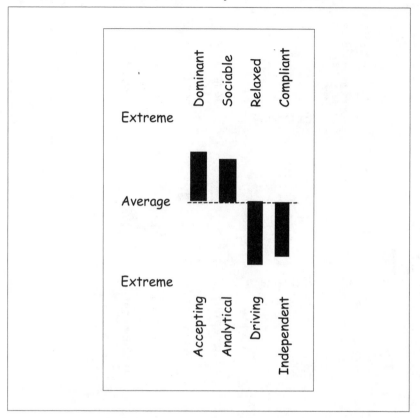

Of course, all of this begs the question, which we put to the boss, "Are your top performers people you are really happy with, or did you just survey the best you had available?" The answer? "We are really happy with the people you interviewed. More important, our customers are really happy with them."

SELECTING SERVICE NATURALS

If money were no object, we would hire a psychologist to interview new job candidates. Everyone would undergo a battery of tests, and if they weren't too worn out after all the poking and prodding, they would work for us happily ever after.

Nothing is going to beat a good profiling instrument when it comes to selecting Service Naturals. But, hey, money doesn't grow on trees,

FIGURE 10.2 *Actual Top-Performing Customer Service Reps*

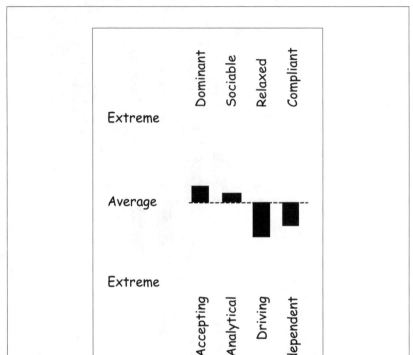

and it makes sense to first separate the wheat from the chaff before you spend your hard-earned dollars on an instrument. By the way, using a behavioral instrument is not an expense; it's an investment.

Those of us who live in the real world need a better idea. The better idea is simple, not necessarily easy. Great interviewers want to know one thing: Will this person do the job? Not *can* but *will* the person do the job? The problem is twofold. First, you have to get good candidates through the door to begin the selection process. Recruiting is a marketing problem. You have to be seen as the employer of choice rather than the employer of last resort. An acquaintance, who seems to be forever hiring, once told me, "How could I possibly respect anyone who would work here?" Got any idea why he was constantly hiring?

To get great applicants in the door, treat the great employees you already have as if they were customers. Three things are likely to happen:

1. Retention will improve, and you will have to hire fewer new folks.
2. Your great employees will become your living testimonials that this is a great place.
3. Winners hang out with winners; employees' friends will apply.

Getting applicants back out the door. Unfortunately, we are often so glad to get anyone to apply that we forget one of the main purposes of the interview—that is, to disqualify the candidate. Because of the high likelihood that a candidate will display what Bill Wagner calls the dating, or interview, personality, our first duty is to break through the best-behavior facade to see what's really there.

An interview should not be about the company or the job or the rest of the team except for what must be revealed to determine fit. Interviews, at least the first two or three, should be treated like what they should be: an investigation. After all, you are taking a big risk, making a huge decision. You are about to invite what is now a total stranger to share your secrets, handle your customers and other valuable assets, and generally expose the entire team to risk. This isn't dating!

PREDICTING FUTURE PERFORMANCE

The sole purpose of an interview is to predict future performance. Wrapped up in the idea of future performance is both *ability* and *fit.* Ability is the combination of natural-born talent and learned skills. Fit is the emotional component that answers the question, Does the candidate like the work and the rest of the team and, of course, does the team like the candidate? Does the candidate have the ability to actually perform the job and have a personality that fits comfortably with the personality of the boss, members of the team, and customers? A valid profile is your best predictor of future behavior, but it's not the only one. Past performance is one reliable predictor of ability, and gut instinct is an incredibly reliable predictor of fit.

But here's the bad news. When it comes to past performance, some questions you can't safely ask. For example, asking for an arrest record is off limits, because certain minorities are arrested in disproportionate numbers. (Being arrested is nothing more than being officially detained. An arrest is not a conviction or proof of guilt.)

"Have you ever been convicted of a felony?" is also a dangerous question. Presumably, a former convict is just that, a *former* convict. Debt to society has been paid, the slate is clean, and unless the conviction was for robbing convenience stores and you are hiring a convenience store clerk, inquiring about criminal history puts you out where the ice is really thin.

We'll concede that there are many questions you can't ask, questions that pretty much match questions you shouldn't ask. Still, aren't you just a tad curious? We are too! So we asked some of the country's best personnel practitioners to discover the 12 most productive (revealing) interview questions.

The Experts Speak

One of our first responses came from Lea Conner. Lea is so gregarious that asking her a question, any question, is redundant. Before she had expended half a breath, we knew she was Irish and not one to mince words. "First describe the job requirements, and then ask, 'Is there any reason you couldn't do this?' Then tell them the work hours and ask, 'Is there anything that might cause conflicts in meeting this schedule?

"We don't care if applicants are married or practice some weird religion. We just want to know if they can do the freakin' job! So tell 'em they have to lift 500 pounds and juggle donuts . . . and they'll let you know if they can or can't." Are we clear, sports fans?

When Mel Chasen, author of *Entrepreneurship* (*Made EZ*, 2002), was hiring key executives, he liked this question: "Everyone you gave as a reference will most likely say good things. If I were to call someone whom you recommended and asked that person to name a weakness, what might that answer be?"

Rex Mudge is a tad more analytical. Although his questions are open-ended and don't appear to be tightly focused, Rex knows exactly what he is looking for. We paraphrased a bit: When looking for relationship building, creativeness, customer service orientation, adaptability, and resourcefulness, "Tell me about your most successful customer-related situation. Why was it so successful?"

When looking for adaptability, resourcefulness, creativity, and innovation, "Tell me about the worst situation you have had to deal with regarding a customer service situation. Why was it difficult and what did you have to do out of the ordinary to satisfy the customer?"

When seeking to verify that applicants have the experience to back up the rhetoric and are representative of solid customer relations skill, "Tell me about your approach (philosophy) toward serving your customers. Now, give me two examples to support your contention."

When checking if applicants' experience has an influence on their methods of handling situations, adaptability, and learning from mistakes, "What is your biggest work-related regret and why? What was the situation, what did you do, and what resources did you employ? Could it have been done differently in retrospect with a different outcome?"

Rex says most of these questions can be modified to seek out different skills or competencies—managerial skills, project management skills, and leadership qualities. Try to develop two or three behavioral examples to support each skill. This allows you to see if the examples are consistent and high-achieving or if the applicants are riding on one great example (home run) and two average examples.

"I forward applicants a list of competencies (skills) that I am looking to discuss with them so they are better prepared (or at least should be) and won't be surprised during the interview. I try to instruct them about the interview protocol and process as much as possible to help ease their anxiety. It's not a game of attempting to stump them as much as an opportunity for them to bring out their best. I would hate to have a wonderful applicant in front of me who, for whatever reason, didn't have the chance to show his or her A game."

John L. Naples, president of Encore Consulting Group (www.en coreconsulting.net) has interviewed hundreds of potential candidates and has come up with a few questions that are both revealing *and* legal. Here is a favorite: "What can you do for us that other candidates can't?"

Carole Martin, The Interview Coach (www.interviewcoach.com), coaches job seekers in the San Francisco Bay area and is a contributor to <www.interviewMonster.com>. Carol says, "Behavioral questions are best, because they reveal more information such as 'Tell me about a time when . . .' or 'Give me an example.' Asking for specific experiences is better than asking 'What would you do if . . . ?' where they can spin a tale."

Two of Carole's favorites: "Why do you want to work for this company?" followed by "What do you know about this company?" and "Do you have any questions?" Listen to what they ask . . . they should show an interest, according to Carole. "An interview," says Carole "should be a conversation."

Colleen Kay Watson of Career Professionals likes to ask, "Tell me about the most challenging and least challenging thing you have ever done," and "Tell me about the last time that you made a major change." She follows these with "Why did you do it? How did it work out?"

THE POWER DOZEN

I'll make it easy for you. Here are the 12 all-time most revealing interview questions:

1. Question: Is there any reason you could not do this job?
   Reveals: Ability to meet job requirements.
2. Question: Is there anything that could conflict with this schedule?
   Reveals: Conflicts that might make it difficult to be present and on time.
   Follow-up: In your previous job, what scheduling conflicts did you encounter?
   Reveals: Potential past conflicts and possible reasons for termination.
3. Question: What motivates you?
   Reveals: Fit.
4. Question: Tell me about a time when you had to violate company policy.
   Reveals: Previous breaches of ethics as well as policy. May also reveal a very desirable trait of using judgment and putting the customer first.
   Follow-up: What were the circumstances and the results?
   Reveals: Depth of commitment.
5. Question: If I ask your references for a weakness, what will they say?
   Reveals: Likely to bring to light personal weaknesses.
6. Question: What was the best customer service interaction you ever had?
   Reveals: Potential fit.
7. Question: What was the worst customer situation you ever had?
   Reveals: Potential fit.
8. Question: What is your biggest work-related regret?
   Reveals: Motivation, past conflicts, breaches of ethics.
9. Question: What can you do for us that the other candidates can't?
   Reveals: Salesmanship, personality, and style.

10. Question: How would you respond if (job situation) happened to you?
    Reveals: Style, fit, attitudes.
11. Question: Tell me why you are wonderful.
    Reveals: Personality, fit.
12. Question: Why do you want to work for this company?
    Follow-up: What do you know about this company?
    Reveals: If candidate did his or her homework, depth of interest, and commitment.

Bonus Round:
    Question: What is the one question I should have asked but didn't?
    Reveals: Areas of potential concern or deception, salesmanship.
    Question: Do you have any questions?
    Reveals: Motivators, level of research, fit.

THE RANGING QUESTIONS

If you ask the power questions listed above and pay close attention, chances are you'll pick up the cues you need to estimate how an individual's personality might profile. You can literally sketch out a profile graph, draw in a few bars, and should know from your verbal interview whether it makes sense to proceed with an online or paper profile instrument if you have done your homework and created a composite profile for each job.

We took the following four questions from the people at the McQuaig Institute®. These are only 4 of more than 100 behavioral questions that are generated by this system. If you aren't certain about the profile, try these four ranging questions:

1. *Tell me about a time when you were involved in a competition.* (Looking for dominant or accepting response; is the response appropriately balanced?)
2. *Tell me your thoughts about how employees should interact with customers.* (Looking for sociable or analytical response; Service Naturals will be friendly but remain focused on business)

Work environments can be relaxed or rushed. Which do you prefer? Why? (Looking for relaxed or driving response; will this person respond well in busy periods?)

What are your thoughts about following rules? (Looking for compliant or independent response; Service Naturals know which rules should be challenged and which rules must be followed exactly)

The Peanut Butter Question

What makes an interview question a great interview question? Predictability.

> **T** *h i n k i n g* **P** *o i n t*
>
> *The art and soul of employee selection is based on the belief that past behavior predicts future performance.*

Discrimination is the purpose of an interview. We're talking legal, ethical, and moral discrimination. You are attempting to separate the wheat from the chaff, the good from the bad, the reliable from the no-shows, and that is a form of discrimination. No matter how well intentioned you may be, you are walking a legal minefield of federal regulations that presume your intentions are evil and that the thief or druggie or whatever is attempting to get on your payroll, close to your assets, and is a mere victim of society in need of protection.

Screw up the interview, and you'll quickly discover that one of the hallmarks of American jurisprudence (the idea that you are presumed innocent until proven otherwise) does not apply to employers charged with discrimination.

Discrimination is illegal on the basis of race, color, creed, national origin, religion, age, sex, and disability (including substance abuse and in some places weight, height, criminal history, and sexual preference). Not to worry. None of the above categories makes much difference when it comes to the ability to turn in a good day's work. Discrimination is legal for reasons of sloth, dishonesty, rude behavior, failing to show up as scheduled, and all those other irritations that make employers nuts.

So what's an employer to do? Well, to start you have to avoid the seemingly innocuous questions such as "Do you have a car?" You think you are asking a simple question when, in fact, you are just about to hang yourself! It doesn't matter that your office is in the boonies and miles from public transportation—you can't blurt out such an invasive question! But you can ask, "Do you have reliable transportation?" How they get to work is none of your business and asking about vehicle ownership could be considered discriminatory (certain racial groups might be less likely to own a vehicle; therefore, the question is discriminatory.)

Better to ask an applicant about peanut butter. What makes a question okay or not is whether it predicts a behavior that relates to a bona fide occupational qualification (BFOQ). The parishioners of a Catholic church might legitimately inquire of a potential new priest if he is a male and a Catholic—BFOQ. Hooters Restaurants lost a squeaker when they failed to prove that looking good in tight shorts and a crop top (and being female) was important to serving hot wings and beer—not a BFOQ.

So, peanut butter.

What if you had 200 store managers and discovered that 49 of the 50 most profitable stores were run by managers who reported that peanut butter was always a part of their breakfast? And what if you discovered that not a single one of the managers of the 50 least profitable stores reported a penchant for peanut butter? You'd want to know, wouldn't you?

You might feel silly. You might ask your assistant to do the asking. But, by golly, you wouldn't be hiring too many peanutphobics, would you?

> **T** h i n k i n g **P** o i n t
>
> *What makes an interview question valid is*
> *its ability to legally predict future behavior.*

POLYVIEWING

I'll bet you didn't know that at most restaurants the employees are expected to pay for their meals. Employee's meals are usually priced at a reduced rate—the norm for fast-food restaurants is half price—but they still must pay.

When Buns and I ran a fast-food fried chicken franchise, we couldn't stomach the idea that the day before payday our near-minimum-wage employees could find themselves surrounded by the sight and smell of mountains of good food but maybe not have enough change in their pockets to afford even half-priced fast food. So the rule was, "Eat what you want when you want, and as much as you want but never, ever graze or take food to go."

In a quick-service restaurant you inventory everything except tap water. I had just finished counting the pecan pies in the cooler when I was called to the phone. A moment later I noticed an employee slip into the cooler. I turned to watch him leave, and when he noticed me watching, he tried to hide something small in the hand furthest from me. His next move was to head straight for the restroom. In a matter of seconds the door reopened and he was back to work.

Something wasn't right. We continued with closing and all left the building at the same time. But something bothered me, so I unlocked the back door, stepped into the restroom, noticed the trash had not been emptied, and dumped the contents onto the floor. I found used paper towels, empty drink cups, and—a wrapped pecan pie. A pecan pie? I left the building and fired an employee. But not for a pecan pie, for dishonesty.

An employee who will steal a pie will steal anything. It just takes more effort to justify the larger theft. Wouldn't it be nice if applicants would come right out and admit to past lapses of integrity? Well, they will, but you have to ask. Actually, you have to ask just right. We were amazed to discover that applicants will admit to theft, even the use of illegal drugs while at work if you know how to ask.

I know what you're thinking, "No one in their right mind would blow a chance at a new job by admitting to a sullied sense of integrity." Good! I'm glad you think so. It indicates that perhaps you have nothing to hide! It also helps to make my point that honest people think differently from dishonest people. Smart interviewers can take advantage of the difference. The technique is what we call *a contrasting setup;* around the office we refer to it as *polyviewing.* If you want to become an expert in the technique, we recommend that you contact the Reid Company at <www.reid.com> for its version of the technique.

Here's a typical contrasting setup: "We're not looking for perfect people, but we are looking for honest people. It's not uncommon for people to take small things without permission and sometimes forget to give them back. So what would you estimate to be the total value of things you might have taken without permission and forgotten to return over the past few years?"

Keep reading . . . we'll show you how it works! In his landmark book *Influence: the Psychology of Persuasion* (Quill, 1998), Robert Cialdini introduces the principle of contrast. Cialdini says that truth is often a matter of perception and perspective and that a fact or an idea often takes on value relative to what it may be positioned against. (These are my words, not his.) "There is a principle in human perception, the contrast principle, which affects the way we see the difference between two things that are presented one after the other. Simply put, if the second item is fairly different from the first, we will tend to see it as more different than it actually is." (Those are his words!)

It is the contrast principle that the Reid Company takes advantage of to wring a surprising amount of what you might consider sensitive information from job applicants. The idea behind the Reid method is to juxtapose a little slip of integrity against a large slip of integrity. It works for one simple reason: Dishonest people don't think like you and I!

Take another look at the setup. "We're not looking for perfect people." This says if you're perfect, we don't want you! "But we *are* looking for honest people." Implied is that you should at least tell us something to demonstrate that even though you aren't perfect (which we implied was okay), you are at least forthcoming.

"It's not unusual for people to borrow things without permission and forget to return them." Now, this should sound like theft to you because it is. To a thief it won't sound at all out of the ordinary. "There's a big difference between running a few copies for the Little League and walking off with the day's deposit." Here is contrast at its finest! "So what would you estimate—and be fair to yourself—might be the total value of everything you might have borrowed without permission and forgotten to return over the past two or three years?" We say be fair to yourself as if we expect that applicants would give us a much larger number.

Here's what you can know for sure: Whatever the number they give you isn't the entire truth. So it's good to follow up by suggesting other ways they may have slipped. "Okay, so you took a couple of pencils, ran Little League flyers on the copier, and used the company phone to call your mom every afternoon. What would you say would be the total value over the course of a year?" Wait for the answer and then dig a little deeper. "I appreciate that. Were there ever any other instances, such as maybe being given something to take home by someone who perhaps wasn't authorized to give it?"

Get the concept? If the difference between the first amount and the second is small, and you can live with it . . . go ahead with the interview. But if the difference is large, you may be seeing only the tip of the iceberg. Once an applicant has exceeded whatever amount is your personal limit, there is no need to keep digging. The interview is about protecting your company, not saving the universe!

For our purposes we make two comments. First, if you don't make integrity a part of your interview, you are nuts; and, second, you don't need a polygraph, torture, or truth serum to learn all you need to know to make a hiring decision. But here's comment number three: Nobody is perfect. And if you can't accept that, don't use the contrast interviewing technique. You won't be able to hire anyone, and you will end up old, crazy, and working the entire company by yourself!

You could use the contrast technique to probe on-the-job use of debilitating substances. But be careful. Stay legal. Thank goodness, Congress or the "Supremes" have not yet declared theft a disability!

I dug out a couple of 20-year-old videos to provide the following not quite verbatim transcript of my first interview using the contrast principle. The applicant's name was Dan. He was a former employee—a supervisor—at a plant making jeans.

> TSG: "What was the reason you left?"
>
> Dan: "I was fired." [Surprise! It turns out the dishonest often use partial truths to cover the whole truth.]
>
> TSG: "Tell me why."
>
> Dan: "I was fired because I did not want to be responsible for closing up the plant at night. I already had too many job duties. When I told my plant manager, he said then he didn't need me."
>
> TSG: "Was there anything that led up to this?"
>
> Dan: "Well, the day before I had a disagreement with my payroll supervisor, and that's what led up to it."
>
> TSG: (Pause)
>
> Dan: "When I got there she . . . I told her that the keys she had assigned me didn't fit, and I couldn't lock up the gate. She wanted me to try the keys, and I told her I didn't have time. I could come back after I got my people working. She told me that if I didn't want to do it, then I should not expect to walk out with a job. That's what she told me. I told her I could do it later, that I was voluntarily taking care of the plant and she should do me a favor and let me come back when I had time, but instead she called the plant manager, and they called me in the office and that's when they brought everything up."
>
> [This was my first use of contrast, so I totally blew an opportunity to follow up on a clue as big as a house—"that's when they brought everything up."

On reflection, not catching the clue probably saved the interview, because I got to the contrast setup and here's how things unfolded.]

TSG: "Thanks for being honest about being terminated. Most people have done these things and simply forget to put them on the application as we just saw about your termination [we're making him feel like one of the gang] and again we aren't looking for perfect people, just honest people, and I remind you that there's probably nothing you can tell me that I haven't heard or even done myself. So in any of your previous jobs, have you had the opportunity to handle money?"

Dan: "In any of my previous jobs have I had the opportunity to handle money?" [He looked away to repeat the question which is a classic stall routine. Here comes a big one!]

TSG: "Sometimes people borrow money from the till without permission to get a cup of coffee or a soda and forget to pay it back, and that's not quite in the same league as walking away with the deposit [contrast], so give me an estimate, and be fair to yourself, of the total amount of money that you may have borrowed without permission and forgotten to return over the past few years."

Dan: "I don't think I've ever taken any money, sir. As a matter of fact, I know for sure I haven't taken any money. That's one thing I just don't do." [What I am dying to discover is what *do* you do! But I wait for the moment.]

TSG: "Not even for a coke or something small?"

Dan: "No sir, I have never taken money from companies. I have never done that. It's one thing I do not do."

TSG: "So what do you do?"

Dan: "Maybe a pencil here or shake a machine for a free soda, but money I do not do."

TSG: "Borrowing change for a soda is not the same as backing a truck up to the loading dock [again, contrast], so give me an estimate of the total value of anything you may have borrowed without permission and forgotten to return over, say, the past two years."

Time Out: Two key points are of concern when it comes to theft or any other lapse of integrity. First, you want an estimate of the wrongdoing *but* you never accept the first amount without probing further. An applicant may toss you a bone to see what you will accept. You don't really care what the truth is; you care only about the *magnitude* of the truth. And if someone goes from a little to a whole lot more in one easy step, chances are you are seeing just the tip of the iceberg.

Second, you don't care what amount of the indiscretion is the actual amount. Once the applicant has surpassed whatever you deem acceptable, you don't need more gory details.

Dan: "Well, let me explain this. It's my job to make sure that people don't take things. We have a supply room, and they give me permission to get in there and get whatever I need; and I do have permission to get whatever I need, so if I backtrack to . . . " [He talks about two previous jobs before I bring him back to the latest job. Does his mention here of the supply room relate to the payroll supervisor wanting to check which keys he has?]

TSG: "Yes, but I was wondering if you could give me a number. And don't inflate it. Be fair to yourself."

Dan: "In those five years I was there, I would say maybe ten pens . . ."

TSG: "In terms of dollars?"

Dan: "Maybe a dollar something, a pen. So $10."

TSG: "Did you ever borrow or maybe were given something that wasn't authorized, merchandise that was extra or damaged or something like that?"

Dan: "I took a couple of pants out of the company."

TSG: "A couple of pants?"

Dan: "Well, we had a system where we sew our own pants, and we can take them out or I can . P. . I do this on my own time, and I can use the machines and the material to produce a pant. So I walk out of there with a pair of pants. I made them and I took them, and if I had to, I could get someone to sign that I had permission. And we had this system until another supervisor was making pants for the operators and that's when they put a stop to it. It was for our benefit, only for supervisors . . . "

TSG: "And was this system kind of informal?"

Dan: "It was to show that we liked the pants that we made instead of some other brand. It wouldn't look good if we walked out of there wearing some other pants."

TSG: "Was this an authorized practice?"

Dan: "Yes, until the other supervisor was caught."

TSG: "And would you say that you continued the practice even after that?"

Dan: "Yes, because I felt that as long as I was not giving the pants to the operators, it wasn't really hurting the company."

TSG: "So how many pairs of pants did you take after the practice was stopped?"

Dan: "I would say . . . six?" [He asked this question as if prefaced by "Would you believe?"]

TSG: "And how much would you estimate to be the total value of those pants?"

Dan: "Well, pants are expensive so $35 times five is $175, but I helped the company out a lot, just a pair of pants here and there."

TSG: "Was there any time when someone gave you something that maybe they weren't authorized to give?"

Dan: "No, sir, it was my job to see that people didn't take things."

Now I could have ended the interview right here by saying, "Geez, Dan! You're a regular little thief." That of course would be unfair, judgmental, and totally stupid. Once you have decided that this isn't the right applicant, continue on to other, more neutral topics and then politely say, "We'll call you if you are the candidate we select." Never, ever refuse to hire someone for something that you cannot, but don't need to, prove. If asked, the answer is always "We found someone we felt was better qualified."

Where, Oh, Where?

Does it really matter where or how you ask an interview question? Some say it does. A fabled story reports that Henry Ford liked to interview executives while at dinner. The story goes that if the executive salted his food, that would be it for Henry, not to mention an astonished candidate!

Some say visiting a candidate at home reveals much about his or her character. Others say simply walking candidates to their car tells you plenty about their lifestyle. (Stop whining! I know asking candidates if they have a car is illegal, and not hiring someone because he or she doesn't have a car is discrimination, not to mention wrong.)

HIRING STEP-BY-STEP

The first step in hiring is to define the job—in behavioral terms! It's not the lack of education or experience that torpedoes employees. Most job failures have nothing to do with ability and everything to do with fit.

We rarely need rocket scientists in the service industry. Rocket science is a matter of education and skill. Serving guests, patients, clients, members, or patrons is a matter of fit. Great service is more will-do than can-do. If you manage to hire a great employee without first defining the job, count yourself lucky, not good. How can you recognize a good candidate if you haven't defined what a good candidate is?

I believe that even though there's a right job for almost everyone, almost everyone is in the wrong job. Just because you have a full bus doesn't in any way imply that you've done a good job in hiring.

Be careful when defining the job. Sales or service is simply too broad a category. Does the sales position require generating leads or simply answering the phone? Are you selling low-cost impulse items or big-ticket items? Does service require establishing a relationship or simply performing some minor service?

Following are questions you can ask yourself that will help you define the job:

- What are the main job duties, and how much time is spent on each?
- How will you determine success?
- How does this position fit into the overall organization?
- What is the working environment in terms of people, details, and amount of supervision?
- What makes this job difficult?
- What makes this job desirable?

All of the questions above will move you in the right direction, but it is the next exercise that rings the bell: *List the behaviors required of this job.* There's no need to be fancy; just list the skills and behaviors required for success, as shown in the following example.

Fast-food server:	Dependable, reasonable appearance, able to count, works quickly
New-car salesperson:	Self-reliant (depends on commissions), detail oriented
Fine-dining server:	Attentive to guests' needs, able to upsell
Medical receptionist:	Attentive to details, pleasant, good communicator

Most important is that you examine the job before you even think about interviewing candidates! Match the employee to the work. Check out the four graphs in Figure 10.3 depicting four candidates for a tech support job. Refer to Figure 10.2 on page 80 and to Figure 10.3. The first three applicants show their natural style; the fourth is what a Service Natural in this particular job looks like. Which of the three candidates could sustain the behaviors required with the least amount of stress and the understanding that any personality could exhibit the perfect personality for the job? Notice how easily you can make this decision visually.

Stress is the leading cause of employee turnover. Some HR professionals say that job-related stress stems from poorly defined expectations and insufficient support. Maybe. The more likely source of employees' on-the-job stress is their attempting to do something or be someone that just isn't them.

HIRING DECISIONS

Bill Wagner says about a third of our hiring decisions are good decisions, another third are minimally effective, and the remaining third are miserable failures. Take a quick look at your own team and mentally calculate your average. Or here's an interesting test: Which member of your team is most likely to call in sick either just before or just after a holiday? Did a name instantly come up? If it did, that's the one who has to go!

FIGURE 10.3 *Job Candidates for Tech Support versus Tech Support Service Natural*

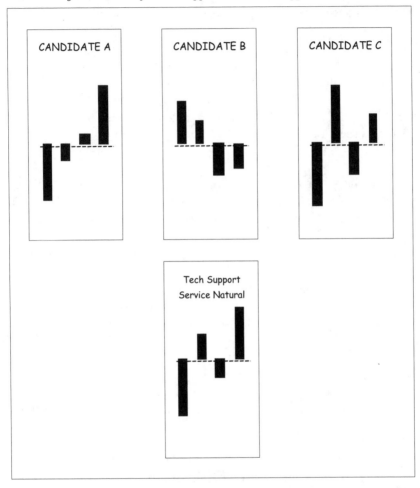

Here's why your hiring decisions don't work out: You are basing your decisions on the wrong information. Check out the three levels of appraisal:

Level I	**Level II**	**Level III**
Appearance	Knowledge	Attitudes and beliefs
Manners	Acquired skills	Self-motivation
Expressiveness	Training	Stability and persistence
Interests	Experience	Maturity and judgment
Goals	Education	Aptitude/capacity to learn
Credentials	Temperament/personality patterns	

Source: The McQuaig Institute of Executive Development, Ltd., Toronto, Canada, 2003.

FIGURE 10.4 *Three Levels of Appraisal*

	Ease of Appraisal	Is Appraisal Objective or Subjective	Changeable or more Stable	Impact on Performance
LEVEL I Appearance	Easy	Subjective	Changeable	Low
LEVEL II Skills	Easy	Objective	Changeable	Low/High
LEVEL III Personality	Difficult	Objective	Stable	High

Source: The McQuaig Institute of Executive Development, Ltd., Toronto, Canada, 2003.

Let's evaluate the value of each list in terms of hiring based on four standards: (1) ease of appraisal; (2) objective or subjective; (3) changeable or stable; and (4) impact on performance.

Level I attributes are easy to appraise, very subjective, changeable, and have little impact on performance. Level II attributes are easy to appraise, objective, changeable, and, in the service industry, have little impact on performance. And for the payoff: level III. These attributes are difficult to appraise in a traditional interview; they are objective, highly stable, and have an incredible impact on performance.

So which of the three levels is usually the centerpiece of our hiring? Well, it isn't Level III! As shown in Figure 10.4, there are appearance, skills, and personality; and of the three, *personality* is the one that really counts. Personality determines fit.

UNCOVERING GREAT LEADERS

Great leaders are born, not made. Jim Collins in *Good to Great* discovered that great leaders share certain characteristics. Great leaders, he says, are ambitious for the company, not for themselves; they're modest and driven to produce. The great ones, he says, are workmanlike; more plow horse than show horse. They are also quick to give credit and quick to take blame.

Bill Wagner, as you might suspect, views them as a profile in Figure 10.5.

Looks a lot like the guy who got his wallet back on a Paris subway!

FIGURE 10.5 *Great Leader Profile*

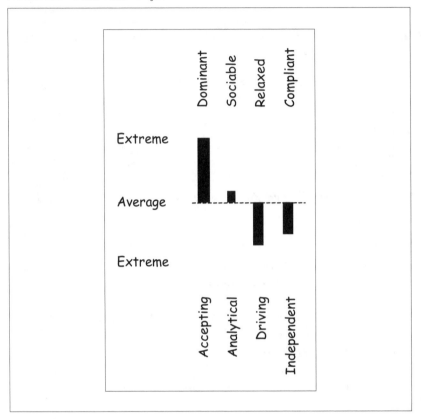

THE BROAD PICTURE

When we surveyed managers for their ideas about the perfect service personality, we discovered two things. First, managers think great servers have huge, larger-than-life personalities. Managers believe that great servers are more than merely sociable; they see them as flamboyant rather than merely friendly. Although a great server should be willing to go to bat for the customer, the boss is thinking in terms of strongminded and persistent rather than simply being willing to question a policy.

Second, the managers, without exception, who helped with our project described the ideal server's personality totally differently from the personalities actually exhibited by their own best servers. What a surprise for them—and us! We weren't surprised, however, to discover that the best servers looked totally different from the worst servers.

FIGURE 10.6 *Boss's Ideal Server vs. Actual Top Performer*

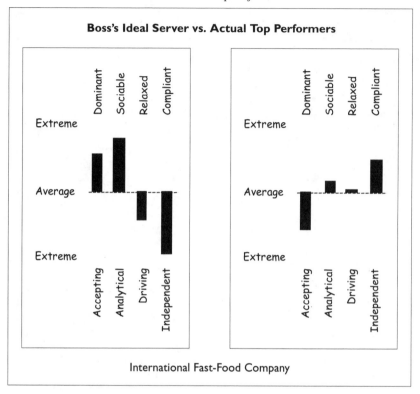

It's safe to say that in most cases we wouldn't recognize a great server if one fell on us. A few examples from three diverse industries to prove my point are shown in Figure 10.6.

Now let's do something fancy and put two arch rivals side by side. Can you tell in Figure 10.7 which is the bank and which is the credit union? (The credit union is on the left!)

FIGURE 10.6 *Boss's Ideal Server vs. Actual Top Performers, continued*

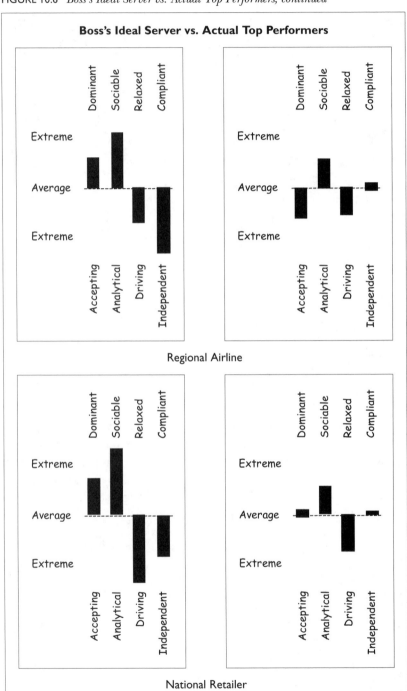

FIGURE 10.7 *Financial Institutions–Boss's Ideal Top Performer vs. Actual Top Performer*

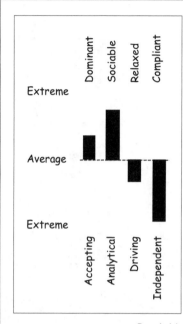

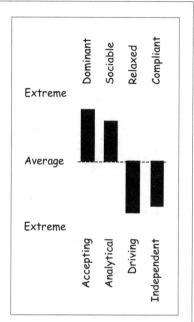

Boss's Ideal Top Performer

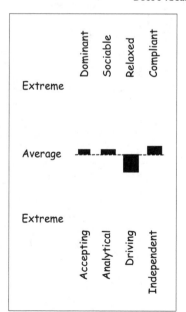

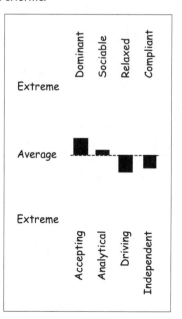

Actual Top Performers

FIGURE 10.8 *Medical Receptionist vs. Emergency Room Staff*

Medical Receptionist   vs.   Emergency Room Staff

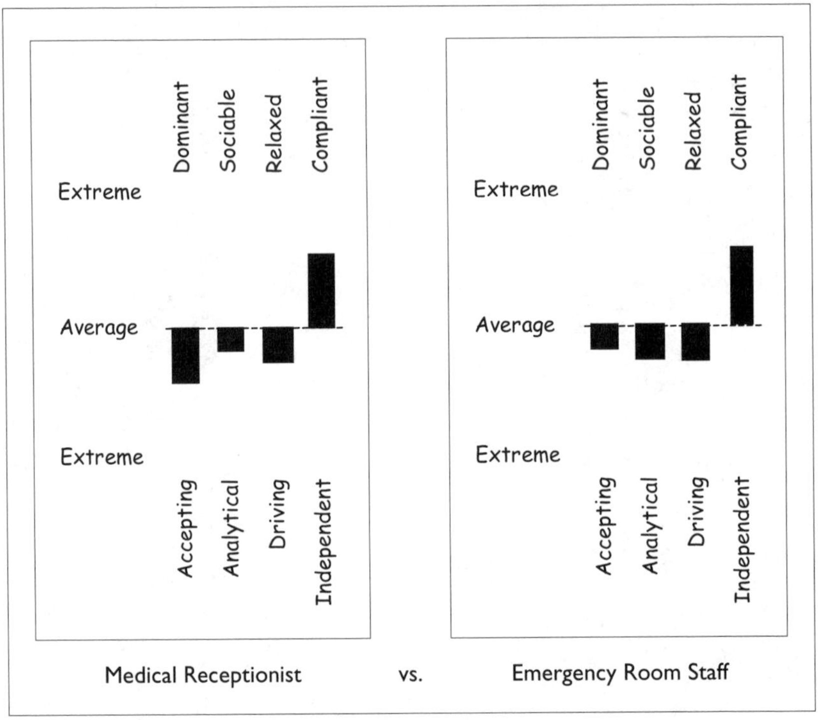

Figures 10.8 and 10.9: A Few Fun Comparisons!

Personality Traits of Medical Receptionist

Good with detail
Accepting, cautious, deliberate
Restless, sense of urgency
Average sociability
Doesn't want to supervise

Personality Traits of ER Staff

Good with detail
Logical, work oriented, analytical
Restless, sense of urgency
Average competitiveness
Doesn't like routine work

FIGURE 10.9 *Fast-Food Server vs. Fine-Dining Server*

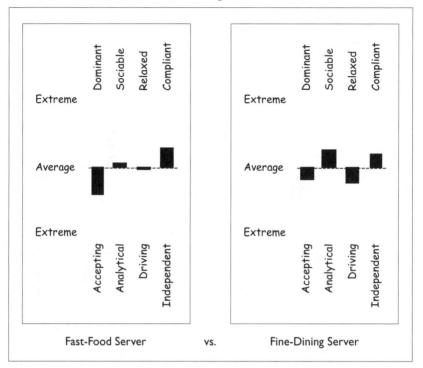

Personality Traits of Fast-Food Server

Accepting, cautious, deliberate
Avoids friction
Follows rules and directions
Careful about making decisions

Personality Traits of Fine-Dining Server

Friendly, outgoing
Optimistic, positive
Follows rules and directions
Prefers working with people

Here's my favorite! See Figure 10.10: WWII Bomber Pilot vs. WWII Fighter Pilot

Personality Traits of Bomber Pilot

Conscientious, cooperative

Good with detail, serious
Logical, analytical
Works best when supervised

Personality Traits of Fighter Pilot

Competitive, goal oriented, ambitious
Enjoys overcoming obstacles
Restless, driving, energetic
Dislikes routine and supervision

FIGURE 10.10   *Bomber Pilot vs. Fighter Pilot*

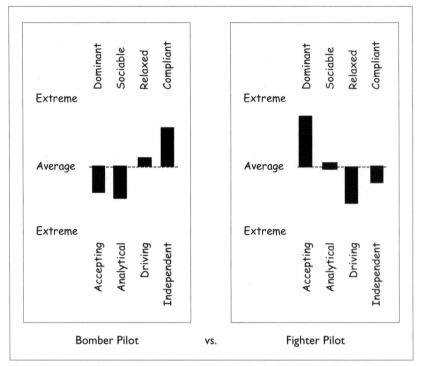

Bomber Pilot   vs.   Fighter Pilot

Finding "Somewhere"

As you can see from the preceding figures, there seems to be a right "somewhere" for everybody. If you want a safe, stable ride, you should look for a bomber pilot. If upside down is your thing, a fighter pilot is whom you want in the cockpit!

Each of the profiles above was different, yet each represented the Service Natural *in each one's industry*. That tells us that a service success in one industry could easily be a service failure in another industry or even in another part of the same industry.

DOES IT REALLY WORK?

One of the pioneers of personality profiling, Herb Greenberg of Caliper, Inc., contends in *How to Hire and Develop Your Next Top Performer* (McGraw-Hill, 2003) that "age, sex, race, formal education, and even experience are invalid predictors of sales success." We'll take the logical leap and presume that the same is true for customer service.

FIGURE 10.11   *Service Natural*

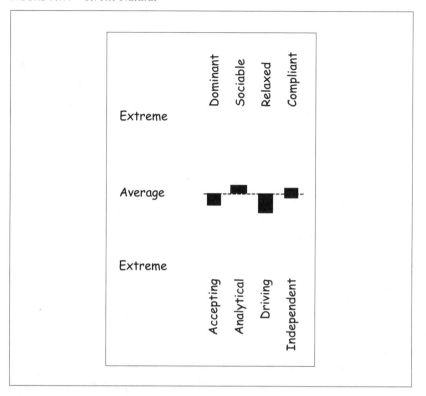

What *will* predict success is the ability to match the personality with the job. A landmark study by Greenberg, published in the *Harvard Business Review* (Sept.–Oct. 1980), discovered that 61 percent of the employees studied who were job matched became top performers within 14 months, whereas only 7 percent of those not matched made it to the top. To put it another way, employees who are matched to the job are eight to nine times more likely to succeed!

Here's a bonus: successful employees stay. In the same Greenberg study, only 28 percent of the job-matched employees were no longer with the company after 14 months, whereas a whopping 57 percent of the unmatched group had punched out. It figures.

T h i n k i n g   P o i n t

Employees should remove the stress of acting out an attempted personality, and they'll find work is more comfortable.

CLASSIC PROFILES

This chapter began with a disclaimer that no single best profile exists for every situation. The only truth is that there *is* a best profile for any given situation. That said, the three profiles at work in every service transaction are, as already noted, Service Naturals in addition to Service Natural Customers and Service Natural Leaders.

Service Natural Customers

Customers who are likely to get great customer service would, for the most part, be described as warm and friendly. But just as no one personality will succeed at delivering great customer service, no one customer personality is going to win every time.

As a generalization, persons likely to inspire servicepeople to give great service will be more accepting than dominant, as no one wants to be pushed or bullied into delivering great service. Customer behavior should tend toward sociability but not be so extreme that servers feel they are being manipulated. Customers should be relaxed. And this one may surprise you—customers should be compliant in most service situations. Why? Because gratuitously asking to break the rules or routine creates unnecessary stress for the server, who has to face the boss after the customer has gone.

If you want to consistently get great customer service, the person to be is depicted in Figure 10.12: the Service Natural Customer.

Service Natural Leaders

Bosses who inspire teams to perform Positively Outrageous Service tend slightly to dominance. They won't look for conflict, but when faced with a decision, they make it without undue hesitation. They

FIGURE 10.12 *Service Natural Customer*

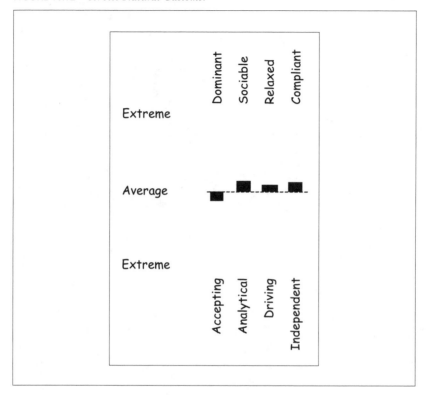

know quality and expect quality, and they balance those expectations with just enough sociability to take the edge off.

Service Natural Leaders are driving, often serving as the energy source when the team is tired or loses focus. And, finally, Service Natural Leaders are slightly independent; after all, they are likely to have bosses too. Still, they are just independent enough to recognize and act when the rules don't fit the situation.

If you could hire only one kind of manager, hire this one, as depicted in Figure 10.13. And, of course, if you could take only a single shot at hiring a customer service person, hire the Service Natural as profiled in Figure 10.11.

FIGURE 10.13   *Service Natural Leader*

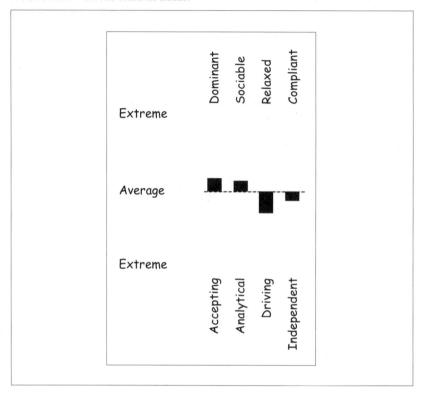

USES FOR PROFILING

Profiling is a useful tool anytime you are considering a new hire, a promotion, or a substantial change of duty, even in the case of a potential termination.

A great employee in one position might well be a complete dud in another. As we discovered earlier, leadership and followership are two distinctly different skill sets. It does not necessarily follow that a top performer in one position in his or her department has the behaviors necessary for success as the leader of that department.

A surprising use of profiling is in the case of a potential termination. Although personalities are not likely to change significantly over time, job requirements often do. A person ideally suited to a position when hired could easily find himself out of place as the job itself continues to change.

We hinted earlier at the differences between real and attempted personalities. Remember the discussion of the dating personality? All of us are capable of exhibiting personalities that are different from our natural selves, but though this is a helpful ability in the short term, it can have disastrous consequences if sustained over the long haul.

Sustaining an attempted personality that is substantially different from the real creates stress. The longer we sustain an attempted personality, the greater the stress. The greater the difference between real and attempted behaviors, the greater the stress.

What this means is that if you mishire, eventually your error will surface. It also means that the happiest workers (those that are least stressed) are those whose personality naturally fits the requirements of the job.

You do no favors for anyone when you hire a candidate in spite of poor fit!

T h i n k i n g **P** o i n t

Have you carefully defined in behavioral terms
the desired personality for each job position?

T h i n k i n g **P** o i n t

Have you committed to profiling in each of the three circumstances:
hiring, promotion, consideration of discipline or termination?

For a closer look at the profile of a Service Natural, please visit <www.tscottgross.com> and follow the links.

IT'S ALL ABOUT THE BOSS

11

WHAT GREAT
LEADERS DO!

When a bureau called to report
that one of its clients wanted consulting to improve its customer service,
a project that my company was born to handle, I was surprised to get
the call.

Consulting for the organization, a metropolitan sewer district, is
not what you would call a glamorous assignment, but, hey, at least it recognized that service is important no matter what the product. Immediately I began to think about the service possibilities.

Before I got too deep in thought, the lady from the bureau added
that we would have to submit a proposal. This wasn't a done deal; we
would have to compete for the business. Aha! Now things were going
to get interesting!

When the request for proposal (RFP) arrived, I realized in a heartbeat that we were a far cry from a shoo-in. No, this RFP was a document
bigger than the one I was likely to submit as a final product. It had bu-
reaucracy written all over it, reeking of low-level clerks sitting in dark-
ened rooms hammering out boilerplate documents stuffed with stilted
language, preconceived notions, and stale ideas.

Two pages into the RFP and I knew that we wouldn't want the work.
This proposal and Positively Outrageous Service clashed like stripes on
plaid. But I read on, thinking that maybe someone who loved custom-

ers might accidentally read our proposal and realize that it was time to get religion.

The RFP solicited a bid for providing classroom customer service training. The project was to begin in October and terminate in June. No executives were to be included in the training, but the results were to include a benchmark of the service as well as the transformation of the organization to a service culture. Since when can you order an organizational transformation? How do you create a service culture through classroom training?

The RFP was full of the latest and greatest management buzzwords, liberally sprinkled throughout the text without apparent rhyme or reason other than to impress. It was obvious to me that the training tactics to be used had already been decided, and the project itself was nothing more than training du jour. When the training had been delivered, the organization would yell, "Next!" and it would be on to the next TQFad of the moment.

My response:

> We are responding to your request for proposal with the thought that you may have made a request that is not in the interest of _____ and that this may not be a project in which either party can win. And if we all can't win, we don't want to play.
>
> Changing a corporate culture is not a matter of training sessions. If it were that easy, you could recruit help from the nearest junior college. Changing a culture is a process, not a project. It cannot be scheduled from September to June. To be candid, anyone who tells you otherwise does not have your interests in mind.
>
> Our proposal follows. It is short on paper, long on concept. The appropriate approach is to survey the beast to see what we have on our hands. Then and only then can a final proposal be created. Submitting a proposal that follows the RFP as written is the rough equivalent of asking a doctor to diagnose without seeing the patient.

Proposal

> Two representatives from T. Scott Gross & Company, Inc., will meet with the decision makers of the district. This group will also include the department heads from training and personnel. Each contractor will visit a subdistrict and spend a day in the field working as a member of a work crew (our choice of

crew). We request that the head of personnel and the head of field operations join us for the day.

This process will require two full days: one day in the field, one-half day meeting with field and office personnel, and one-half day meeting with top decision makers. Our report and recommendation will follow within ten working days. It is likely that our role thereafter will be as advisors only.

A culture change comes from within if it comes at all. We knew when we submitted our response there wasn't a prayer that we would get the business because we sensed, correctly, that no way would leadership invest the time to spend a day doing grunt work in the field.

Great leaders go first. They do not lead from the office. Contrast the above story with an experience we had working for Atlantic Southeast Airlines (ASA), a regional carrier feeding Delta hubs. On our way to our first meeting, a gate agent noticed that we were traveling on a company ticket. "Are you going to see Skip?" Real excitement was in the voice. Skip Barnett is the CEO of ASA and to the entire Delta system he seems to be known simply as Skip. The man who instinctively leads from the front doesn't seem to have a bone of pretension.

Skip leads his airline from the cockpit and frequently plays hooky when he learns unscheduled time is available in the regional jet simulator. Skip intuitively knows that great leaders need to understand the mission from the perspective of the front lines. And even though he isn't likely to captain your plane, you can be confident that he could and that his understanding of the real ASA world is creating a huge reservoir of dedication among the troops.

GO FIRST!

It's a simple little leadership secret that you won't learn anywhere else. Tom Peters came close with his "management by walking around." We hit it right on the head with the secret behind "management by *working* around."

As you learned above, Skip Barnett is one example of executives who willingly and frequently walk in the shoes of their business family. The legendary Herb Kelleher of Southwest Airlines is another. Herb is well known for his habit of working as a baggage handler on the busiest travel days. But lest you think it a publicity stunt, here's a story you haven't heard that will convince you management by working around was a genuine expression of Herb's love of his business family.

In the wee hours of a foggy morning in Houston, a Southwest Airlines crew arrived dead tired after a very long day of flying that had been plagued by heavy weather and mechanical delays. The hour was so late that the shuttle bus driver scheduled to take the crew to the hotel had called it quits, figuring the crew wasn't likely to show.

So there they stood, wondering how the last two miles of a very long trip would be completed when a black luxury sedan rolled to a stop just outside the terminal. The trunk popped open and a white-haired gentleman left the car, entered the terminal, and without a word began to load the bags of the bedraggled crew. It was Herb! He was managing, leading by working around.

Recently, the top executives of American Airlines cried mea culpa after it was discovered—in the midst of executives' wringing wage concessions from already underpaid flight attendants allowing the airline to avoid bankruptcy—top executives had suited up a golden parachute worth millions for themselves.

Some of the great captains of industry should be busted to private. At the very least, they should be sentenced to managing by working around. In a free economy there are only two groups of risk takers: entrepreneurs and employees who are working without a net, the true risk takers who make our economy move.

> **T** *h i n k i n g* **P** *o i n t*
>
> *How could you put managing by working*
> *around to work in your business?*

ARE YOU TALKING TO ME?

If I called on the phone and began offering advice, the first thing you would ask is, "Who is this?" Why should listening to customers be any different? No matter the venue—Internet, telephone, mail, or even in person—it is vital to capture key demographic data about consumers. Discover where your customers live and where they shop. Find out where they shop when they aren't shopping with you. Use your imagination.

When you take your Lexus in for service, the dealer hooks it to a computer for a diagnosis. Guess what else your car is revealing about you? A complete profile of your driving habits is sent directly to Lexus engineering to be used in designing future models. Do you think your car is a marketing genius? What about your clothes washer? Yes, another regular tell-all is watching from the laundry room. In Italy, the Merloni Company has created an Internet-ready clothes washer that reports washing habits along with a diagnostic to the manufacturer that can enable an ailing machine to call for help.

Coming soon to a refrigerator, a microwave, an air-conditioning unit, or to you yourself will be an entire army of digital spies designed to help manufacturers listen better.

> **T** *h i n k i n g* **P** *o i n t*
>
> *What can you do today to improve your hearing?*

Listen Up!

When you're a customer who wants something out of the ordinary, don't ask the server. Ask the boss, and you are more likely to get a yes. Bosses tend to insulate themselves from customers, putting the burden of saying no on the servers. (Servers understand they will be "killed" if they attempt to actually exercise the empowerment mentioned in the mission statement.)

So ask the boss, and watch her squirm and wink at the server on the way out the door!

> **T** *h i n k i n g* **P** *o i n t*
>
> *What can your employees say yes to without getting killed?*

Reputation management must be based on a willingness to listen to consumers, understand, and react accordingly. Pete Blackshaw, who built PlanetFeedback.com to serve as a corporate listening post that allows smart brand managers to quickly take the pulse of the market, says companies have to go beyond building a reputation. They must actively plan and act to protect their reputation. If Warren Buffett is right when he says that a strong brand is like a moat around your business, it makes sense to practice a little moat maintenance. And Blackshaw seems to think listening to customers is one of the best ways to do it.

When consumers are asked whom they trust, firefighters, police officers, and teachers are at the top of the ratings. Although it might not be a surprise to know that corporate America and advertisers are two low-rated groups, who would have imagined they would define the very bottom of the ratings! If you're in business, you have to ask yourself, Why? Also ask, Does this apply to us? (Okay, maybe there is another question: What can we do about it?)

Begin by creating a mechanism for listening that is wrapped around a deliberate plan for creating, building, and maintaining your corporate reputation. There is little difference between corporate reputation and brand. A brand is an expectation. When you talk about brand in terms of corporate reputation, you may be seasoning the discussion with overtones of honesty and integrity, but the differences to your customers in differing terms are negligible.

Washout

If there is one great place for listening to customers, it must be the web. And if there is one great example of on-line listening it might be at www.PG.com, the web portal for Procter & Gamble (P&G), the folks who bring you Tide, Crest, and even Ivory. Procter & Gamble thinks that being great listeners is what makes them great marketers. And listen they do! There is even a link to Help Us Create where P&G customers are asked for their advice on making old products better or creating entirely new ones from scratch.

Of course, they provide great content but always in the context of the brand. You can let Stain Detective tell you how to remove almost any stain from almost any surface. And the good folks at Pampers at <www .pampers.com> seem only too happy to share the massive amounts of information they learned from top to bottom about parenting, even though their primary interest was just in bottoms!

Here's a big lesson: Free content may be a huge Internet myth. Consumers know that behind the content lies a brand, so don't hide the brand. It's a turnoff when consumers can't readily tell who is behind the information they're getting. Consumers prefer to visit a branded site if the brand is good. And they like to know their input is valued by a brand they know and trust.

> **T** *h i n k i n g* **P** *o i n t (f o r   c u s t o m e r s)*
> *Your favorite brands are on the Internet, and because they*
> *want to remain your favorite brands . . . they are listening.*
> *Tell them what you think!*

WEIGH IN, PLEASE

If you're going to listen to customers, you had better think about which ones. All customers may be created equal, but they most certainly don't carry equal weight in the marketplace. If you have offended a customer or even received a helpful customer suggestion, wouldn't it be nice to know how much weight those customers carry? Are they regular customers? Are they big spenders? Are they among the small percentage of customers who are considered influentials or early adopters?

Influentials are more likely to influence the products their friends buy or try new products before their friends by a margin of three to two. You want to know which of your customers are most likely to talk while the rest of the market merely listens. Companies that make it easy for customer feedback are perceived as more customer friendly and more deserving of positive word of mouth.

Offer special customers special treatment. Give them an expressway to connect with you. Invite them to join mailing lists, so they can receive insiderlike tips and new product information. Offer them coupon specials and advance purchase opportunities, or invite them to participate in Beta tests and other product development activities.

Invite customers to participate in a conversation, sometimes literally! Check out <www.liveperson.com>, where they assist organizations in setting up chat features for Web sites. A huge movement today is toward automating customer service. The old fax on demand gave way to branched automated phone assistance, which is giving way to online help and its ubiquitous FAQs, or frequently asked questions. Customers are actually coming to appreciate quick, efficient, free help with their most common questions. But when their question isn't one of the FAQs, consumers want to be able to immediately access another level of assistance.

And every company Web site should include an invitation to comment. Once customers believe they have your attention, it's a given that you have theirs. Take advantage of the opportunity and do a little market research while the getting is good. Make customers feel important, and they will quickly volunteer the answers you may not have known needed asking!

Online chat can be offered as an option to automated responses. Here's the funny thing: A chat option has value even when it's not used. Customers appreciate knowing they can interact with a human being if they want to or need to. Give them the option and be surprised at how many happily turn to the automated system.

AND . . .

. . . don't forget to listen to your employees for two reasons. First, they are likely to have wonderful ideas that otherwise might be lost forever or given to the competition. Second, the very act of asking can have surprising, and often positive, results!

Bendix-King has been known for years as the Cadillac of aviation electronics. When we bought our airplane, I was proud to tell admiring fellow pilots that we had an "all-King radio stack," including the latest in King GPS approach-certified navigation gear.

Then a not-so-funny thing happened. A group of sharp engineers developed a color version of the navigator and in the process combined the communication radios in the same unit. But what should have been a cause for celebration turned out to be a bitter disappointment. Management didn't listen, or so the story goes. The engineers walked, not exactly across the street but close. (The across-the-street metaphor makes for a better story.) Whatever the details, the idea wound up at the competitor's business, Garmin, which soon produced the unit and captured the lead in general aviation electronics. That kind of listening has a measurable benefit.

How about this one? We were working with a major supermarket chain determined to improve its customer service. At least that was the goal of my client. The attitude of management seemed to be far different, at least in that particular division. This division was staring in the face strong competition that had moved into the market, steadily stealing market share.

The response by management came late and was limited to repeated rounds of cost cutting. Maintenance budgets were slashed, as was the budget for labor. The employees could have saved the day if only they had been asked. They knew that well-run, fully staffed stores were the answer, but no one at the head shed seemed to want to listen. My client slaved on like Pollyanna on a mission.

During one store visit in search of ideas, we cornered a middle-aged woman in a sharply pressed store uniform working in the deli department and asked her what she thought could be done to turn things around. Our impromptu session was going well until, and you could see it in her eyes, she was startled by a thought. She began to cry. Oh, no! We wanted to be the good guys and crying employees were definitely not on our list. "I'm sorry," said my gentle and quite panicked client. "Whatever we said to upset you, we're sorry. Please tell me what we said." Through the tears and running mascara, a voice said softly, "I've worked for this company nearly 25 years and this . . . this is the first time that anyone has ever asked for my opinion."

> Consultant—several thousand dollars.
> Expenses—a few hundred more.
> Listening—priceless.

Sometimes you have to go on an SOS raid—what we call stamp out stupid—to see if you can discover and then fix instances in which the system is stacked against great customer service. Look for examples where the lack of time, tools, or training is creating problems. Notice instances of talent or tempo having an impact on service. Sometimes you have to go slow to go fast. Other times, a substitution from the bench is all that is needed, maybe even one from the top.

My JFK Experience: The Importance of Training

It was one of those little things you notice when your attention should be elsewhere. My palms were sweating, which was not a particularly good sign for someone piloting a Canadair Regional Jet into JFK Airport for the first time. Actually, this was to be only the sixth time I had landed a jet of any size, so perhaps I could be forgiven a little nervousness. One at a time and hoping my First Officer wouldn't notice, I wiped my hands on my pants.

The sweating actually began at Atlanta's Hartsfield Airport. We were cleared from the gate by ground control, and I could feel every expansion gap in the concrete. It was raining when we left the gate. The rain had turned to a light snow and reduced our visibility by the time we reached the business end of the long east-west runway.

The CRJ200 model is steered with a tiller to the left of the pilot's seat. You can slow it down or bring it to a stop with the hydraulic brakes mounted as extensions to the rudder pedals. Because I was new to taxiing this 47,500-pound monster, every detail fought for my attention. I worried that the weather at Kennedy would be no better. The approach to Kennedy from the west is one of the world's most unusual approaches. Instead of the long, straight-in approach to the bright white rabbit lights aviators set up from the southwest, you visually locate a miles-long curving series of approach lights. Then you follow along the curve until, miracle of miracles, there waits the runway.

It's counterintuitive, but from five miles out I spotted the approach lights, even though neither the airport nor the runway could be seen in the dark night now a few thousand feet above the city. My First Officer, Skip Barnett, CEO of Atlantic Southeast Airlines, called out the altitude in a subtle reminder that vertical navigation was as critical as the visual lockon to the approach lights. I repeated his callout to let him know that, sweaty palms aside, I was right with him, firmly in control. Skip is a good First Officer and an even better leader. It was an honor to have him in the right seat. After all, it was his airplane, figuratively speaking.

We rounded the curve, and the lights of one of the world's busiest airports winked from the darkness. Approach released us to the tower, the tower cleared us to land, and I stole another quick swipe at my pants' legs. "One thousand feet, gear and flaps in the green," Skip continued with the checklist.

From my vantage point, the far end of the runway looked to be all of a block long. Although I knew this was an illusion, it gave me a start. The glide slope indicator was showing a perfect red over white to indicate that our path to the runway was right on the money. The airspeed, thanks to Skip, was also right on the money. My attention switched back to the view through the windscreen with the runway in the window and the red lights at the far end of the runway steady.

The radar altimeter announcing altitude every 10 feet began the countdown beginning at 50 feet. At 10 feet I increased the flare ever so slightly, more by intuition than the numbers. I was, in pilot terms, "sniffing for asphalt," and I was rewarded by the gentle touch of the mains on the runway, right on the numbers and more than a mile from the far end. I had plenty of time to stop but wanted to make the high-speed turnoff. Good pilots can land on the numbers painted on the end of the runway, but great pilots fly all the way to the gate.

"That was awesome!" It was a voice from somewhere behind me. "Do you want to try that again?" I was on the tiller and steering toward the gate. "I think I'd like to stretch after that one!" The lights came up, and Skip and I joined Brian Wilson, our check pilot, on the small deck of the simulator, all $17 million of it. The simulator is so realistic that the first flight pilots take in a real aircraft is also a revenue trip. Even the FAA says I can log the experience in my flight book! Pretty good training, huh? Here's the good news. You don't need a $17 million simulator to simulate serving customers in your operation.

Training is the process of providing multiple experiences in a compressed span of time. It's a great way to increase skill levels. That I'm living is flying proof of that! And forget about taking complexity out of a job. Consider putting it in!

I, for one, wouldn't mind seeing us reengineer the workplace with the intention of *adding* complication to make the job at hand challenging enough to keep regular people from going absolutely bonkers. The added benefit would be that when customers made out-of-norm requests, employees would be able to handle them and would be comfortable with handling them.

Along with the requirement to think, which accompanies a properly engineered job, comes the requirement for management to empower and take a few small risks. Eliminating variance (risk) through standardizing the job process and focusing employees on narrow, mind-numbing tasks is yet another way to offend thinking customers and employees.

> **T** *h i n k i n g* **P** *o i n t*
>
> *When you make jobs so idiotproof that only idiots*
> *can stand to do them, you have no right to*
> *complain about the quality of help!*
>
> **T** *h i n k i n g* **P** *o i n t*
>
> *Few employees are stupid, but a ton are truly ignorant.*
> *Stupid means you* can't *know how.*
> *Ignorant simply means that you* don't *know how.*
>
> **T** *h i n k i n g* **P** *o i n t*
>
> *Stupid you can avoid; ignorant you can fix.*

GETTING EMPLOYEES TO THINK

For all we do to discourage thinking, you wonder why employees think at all! Let's see, cash registers count change (we're afraid we might lose a dime), computers route phone calls (God forbid we have to talk to a customer), and policies for just about everything. Business is so preoccupied with holding on that we are losing a most precious commodity—employees who think.

The punishments that go along with breaking the policies are worse. When you asked for water at a fast-food restaurant, did you notice that slight hesitation? It's because the counter clerk has to account for the missing cup. How about when you buy a pair of socks only to discover they are the wrong color before you get to your car, and the clerk who sold them to you not three minutes earlier demands to see proof of purchase? Is it the clerk or is it the system?

It takes a tremendously competent organization to turn employees loose. Here's the first step: Stop thinking for them.

I learned the second most powerful leadership question from a fellow by the name of Bill Oncken. Bill led a one-man crusade to get managers to stop firefighting, to empower everyone, and to identify, and then act on, the important rather than the merely urgent. He noticed that many times employees would waltz into the boss's office and simply, though subtly, refuse to think by telling the boss they needed help or didn't know how to . . .

Oncken, the wizard, dreamt up an incredibly powerful team-building question. I can see him now, arms folded, eyebrows arched, as he would reply, saying, "Hmmm! That's interesting. Tell me how you are going to solve that problem."

Try it . . . all together now, "Hmmm! That's interesting. Tell me how you are going to solve that problem." Something amazing will happen. Employees will begin to think. Ask Oncken's second most wonderful question often enough, and, miracle upon miracles, employees will stop saying, "Boss, I need help," or "Boss, I don't know how." Instead, they will think!

> **T** h i n k i n g   **P** o i n t
>
> *What are you doing that may discourage thinking?*

PRACTICE MAKES . . .

Nine years ago my son gave me a copy of the Microsoft Flight Simulator. I didn't get much play time, so I installed the program on my notebook computer for those rare times when I would be willing to kill a little time, usually while flying in the back of a commercial airliner. I had no rudder pedals, no yoke, just the computer and four small arrow keys. Needless to say, I crashed a lot! No problem. It's a game. Just reset and go again.

Except there was a problem. After crashing hundreds of times at Meigs Field in Chicago, the default airport for the Flight Simulator program, I was cleared for approach. Only this time I was in a real airplane; it was brand-new and it was mine! I had practiced this landing hundreds of times, and most of them had ended with my depositing a pile of metal on the runway!

Now, attempting to land here in real life, I flew with the baggage of hours of learning how to do it wrong! They say that practice makes perfect. It doesn't. *Only perfect practice makes perfect.* Poor training can be worse than no training!

Have you ever heard of magic-apron training? It's the practice whereby restaurant managers pair new employees with long-term employees so the novices can follow the old hands around to learn the business. That's a bad idea! Why? Because it is just as likely that the poor habits will get passed along with the good ones.

Perfect practice making perfect is also the argument for never delaying training on grounds that if you do, by the time you get around to training employees how to do things perfectly, they will already have crashed a hundred times. They will be experts at crashing, and you'll have bad habits to break.

> **T** *h i n k i n g* **P** *o i n t*
>
> *It's impossible to delay or avoid training, because*
> *employees are learning* something *whether you like it or not!*

12

SELL THE DREAM

Great leaders focus on long-term, big-picture issues, beginning with sharing the vision. Do you know how they do this? If you don't, read on, and we'll look at values, mission, and vision as you've never seen them before!

Every good business has a *mission statement*. Smart individuals have mission statements too. We needed a mission statement for our small restaurant, understanding that people perform better when they know what is expected, where there is a clear sense of purpose about their work.

At first, we tried something approaching normal: "Have fun serving the finest food in a clean, safe environment where everyone is treated like a friend." Whew! We quickly discovered that even this comparatively short mission statement was too cumbersome.

Normal folks need ideas they can wrap their arms around. So we threw out convention and took a risk. Our corporate cry became "Don't forget to love one another." We even took to ending our radio commercials with "See you at Church's . . . and don't forget to love one another."

"You can't do that!" was what I heard from my consultant friends. "It's too mushy! It may not even be legal!" We figured that if the button-down types were unanimously certain we were wrong, then we must be on to something. We had a sign made to hang over our dining room door reminding everyone to love one another: tough construction workers, civil servants, cops, probably would-be robbers, butchers, bakers, and candlestick makers.

Usually, when I left the restaurant, I would tell the crew, "Hey, guys! I hope you get clobbered," which is restaurant talk for "I hope you're busy." It makes the day go faster. "And don't forget to love one another!"

And they did. In an industry where employees come and go through a revolving door, we had surprisingly little turnover. People didn't think that rough restaurant types would go for a touchy-feely work environment, but it turned out that everyone wanted and needed to know that they were loved. And why not feel loved at work, where you spend so many of your waking hours?

Today, our mission statement is "Have fun and make the world a better place." Our crew of professionals frequently sign their e-mail with "Don't forget to love one another." Even my friend Joe Jaeger once signed a message to me with "Hugs!" Then he must have realized what he had written and couldn't resist adding, "You know, the manly type with a slap on the back!"

YOU GOTTA BELIEVE

As a presenter to sometimes as many as a hundred groups each year, you can bet I've seen the worst of corporate "spizz." (There is no good corporate spizz!) This junior version of corporate mission statements can be read as the themes for corporate conventions. You can bet that a conference in Orlando has the word *magic* somewhere in its theme. Las Vegas seems to attract the "New Beginnings" crowd although that theme rightfully belongs to Phoenix.

Corporate mission statements have become so predictable, trite, and thoroughly uninspiring that a Web site too offensive to name was created for what seems like the sole purpose of mocking consultants and the suits that hire them. (Actually, there is no such Web site; it's only an idea reported by *e-company Magazine!*) Here's a test. Read the following mission statements and determine if they are real or computer generated:

- "To enable human achievement and customer success by transforming information technology."
- "To empower corporate value . . . to stay competitive in tomorrow's world." (Compaq owns the first and the computer owns the latter.)

- "To continually pursue global supply chains as well as to quickly develop value-added paradigms." (The computer strikes again!)
- "Our mission is to achieve or enhance clear leadership, world-wide, in the existing or new core consumer product categories in which we choose to compete." Want to guess? Computer? Nope. Gillette.

Companies talk about values and mission because it's the thing to do. But having values statements and mission statements are one thing; living them is quite another. The real kicker is that companies already have company values and missions whether or not they turn them into formal statements.

The real question for you: Are the mission you state and the values touted in the annual report a reflection of reality as seen by the troops?

START ON THE RIGHT FOOT

Several years ago, in an attempt to discover what it is that makes high-performance teams work, I set out on a series of adventures that we named the Borrowed Dreams project. As part of my research I became a member of more than a dozen high-performance teams, some for a day and others for a week or more, but for all of them I actually joined the team and did the work.

One surprising result was that not once did anyone start my experience by saying that this is who we are, this is what we do, and this is why it matters. Not once. And I have a dollar that says the same is true in your organization. People like to be a part of something that is bigger than they are. They like to know how they contribute to the larger picture.

We call the phenomenal oversight of missing out on the opportunity to get employees started off on the right foot "the lost power of the first day." What then should be included on the first day . . . or two or three? In addition to the obvious policy and paperwork review, new team players need to know the values, mission, and vision of the company; they need to see the big picture, including meeting actual customers. And a mentor can share insights to some of their questions: How will I know when I am winning? And where do I go from here . . . and who cares?

The first day sets the tone for all the days that follow. Unfortunately, most organizations fail to put the power of the first day to work.

Did you realize: It is right up front when the new hires decide if there will be a second day? It is right up front when the new hires decide if there is a good fit with the values of the organization? And it is the new hires who determine what the real values are, not the ones announced by the plaque in the lobby but the values actually experienced on the way to finding the restroom or any of the hundreds of first-time experiences with their new company, which is why at least a part of the first day should be spent with the boss.

Stop Mumbling!

Belmont Village, a network of assisted living communities, has an innovative employee orientation program that demonstrates to new employees what it's like to be in your 80s with failing eyesight, unpredictable balance, and dentures. New staff members literally learn to walk, talk, and see as a senior through challenging activities that simulate common senior frailties like foot corns, cataracts, loss of hearing, and swollen gums. Employees place popcorn kernels in their shoes, coat their glasses with Vaseline, and place cotton balls in their ears. They even wear gloves to simulate a diminished sense of touch and loose dentures come in the form of a mouthful of M&Ms.

Even though the program is a natural invitation to wisecrack, it's a wonderful way to teach new staff their part in lovingly assisting seniors to live life to the fullest!

"I'll Have to Use a Lifeline"

(Thanks to Karen Eldridge, director of news and public information at Maryville College in Maryville, Tennessee, for the following.)

When Fayerweather Hall was struck by lightning and burned in 1999, the tapes and textbooks for the college orientation program were destroyed. The training materials weren't replaced because, according to HR Director Jennifer Hunt, the employees didn't like them. The new program, CO-OP (Connecting Our People), is centered on a ropes challenge course designed by Bruce Guillaume of Mountain Challenge, an outdoor adventure education program located on the Maryville College campus.

"I believe you have to touch the mission frequently to constantly be reminded what it's all about, and I didn't think that was happening for staff," Guillaume said.

"CO-OP gave us an avenue and an opportunity to do that." Guillaume often borrows a scene from Lewis Carroll's *Alice in Wonderland* to illustrate the importance of having a plan (a mission) and a sense of direction in life and work. "There's a part in that story where Alice asks the Cheshire Cat which way she ought to go. The cat explains to Alice that her direction depends entirely on where she wants to get. Alice says she doesn't care, so the cat says it doesn't matter which way she goes."

Hunt says, "The road we take is the mission of the college, and we need to have the road as a backdrop to all the decisions we make every day." Maryville College's mission statement reads: "Maryville College prepares students for lives of citizenship and leadership as we challenge each one to search for truth, grow in wisdom, work for justice, and dedicate a life of creativity and service to the peoples of the world."

Program activities range from tennis ball tosses, where employees juggle tennis balls and other surprise objects, to "spiderweb" passes, where employees have to develop a plan for moving each group member through a rope obstacle course with several limitations. After each activity, staff members are asked to draw parallels to their daily work routine. Facilitators ask: "As a college employee, are you more concerned with how you catch the ball or how you hand it off?" "What happened when she dropped the ball?" "Was it difficult for you to trust people to get you through the web?"

"What's really neat is that you have people from housekeeping talking to people from the theatre talking to people from the humanities office," Guillaume said. "That's been memorable." In follow-up sessions, supervisors discuss how lessons learned support the mission of the college, and they have created a booklet highlighting the best practices that all supervisors can use to build a team that is productive, courteous, happy, and conscious of the college's mission.

"It doesn't matter what a person's job is here; he or she has an impact on the mission of the college . . . And CO-OP has reminded us that we're all partners in education," Hunt said. "We're all here for students."

Once Again, from the Top

The prospect is a huge (make that gargantuan) international operator. If I told you its name, you might suck cold air through your teeth and conjure up an image of me as one very happy consultant hauling money to the bank and sticking feathers in my cap. But you would be wrong.

It was a prospect turned into almost a client. And the prospect had called me! The prospect sought me out for my opinion. Spurred on by its CEO, who had read one of my earlier books, *OUTRAGEOUS! Unforgettable Service, Guilt-Free Selling* (Amazon, 1998), all the company wanted me to do was pass the test of a simple conference call before meeting me at the bank!

That was the plan. The conference call was what did me in. I hate conference calls, always have, even before this opportunity-turned-disaster. They take forever to coordinate and wind up dumping a bunch of folks in a room to go one-on-one with a target on the other end of a phone line. You can't tell whom you're talking to and that's the least of the worries. The worst thing is that inevitably some junior-junior exec at the table can't resist playing "Stump the Consultant" so he can look good in front of the boss.

"So, Mr. Gross, how can you help us improve our customer service?" No point in playing softball, so I respond with, "To begin, we're going to make certain you have the right people serving your customers."

Junior replied, "We have the best people in the business already. What else are you going to do?" "We're going to see if those great people of yours are getting the kind of support necessary for great service to happen."

"You need to know, sir, that all of our team members are empowered to do whatever it takes to make the customer happy," said Junior, no doubt smirking and looking to see if the boss was impressed. "You're wrong." (Why can't I be just a tad more circumspect? Why is it that honesty can't have a softer ring to it? Noooo, I have to just blurt out whatever strikes me as true. To heck with a consulting fee that would pave the driveway and buy a new car to run up and down it.)

Well, I thought the phone line had gone dead. You could have heard the Sprint pin drop, so I said, "Gee, I guess I lost track of to whom I was talking. I hope I didn't offend someone with a million shares in the company." I heard what might have passed for nervous laughter, so I plowed right on, saying, "But no matter what, you're still wrong."

Okay, maybe that wasn't laughter I heard, but dang it! I just hate when corporate weenies get so caught up in their baloney that they start to believe it.

"When your team members are faced with an opportunity to do something really out of the box, they aren't thinking about the customer and they aren't thinking about the company. Do you know who they are thinking about?" I paused for a second just in case someone with a brain and a little backbone had slipped into the room by mistake. Seeing that an answer wasn't on the way, I answered myself, saying, "Given the chance to step out of the box, that person has only one thought in mind: Am I going to get killed for this?"

(That's how empowered your people really are. They want to know if they're going to get killed, and they aren't about to risk doing something different unless they have witnessed the boss working out of the box.) "That's why after we verify your point that you have the best team members on the planet, we're going to take a look at their managers." Do I feel a chill? (And that's when I lost them!)

Myths and Realities

The claim: We're a people company.
The test: Show me your training program.
The claim: We believe in our mission.
The test: Show me your orientation program. (How is your culture communicated?)
The claim: We put customers first.
The test: (Answer your phone!) How do you solve problems? Handle returns?
The claim: We're a learning organization.
The test: (Congrats on reading right now!) What have you learned in the past year?
The claim: We're aggressive, trail blazers.
The test: What do you do to encourage risk taking? Show me your failures.
The claim: We're a competent organization.
The test: Are you chain of command only? Are gossip/politics tolerated? How do you solicit employee input? How do you measure customer loyalty?
The claim: We're a hands-on organization.
The test: Does management *work* the trenches?

TELL 'EM!

I spoke to the managers of a large southern restaurant chain and was surprised to see a thoughtfully prepared booklet titled "The Principles for Success." It was the first time I had seen corporate values and mission so clearly defined for the troops. The group goals were listed in easily measurable terms along with the strategy for their achievement. Wow!

For example, goal number three: "We will consistently reward our shareholders." And what was the plan? "Achieve 2 percent real growth in same store sales without increasing the average guest check. Achieve total revenue growth of 20 percent per year." Clear. Measurable. Focused.

There is absolutely zero value in developing corporate values, mission, and vision and even taking the next step of likening them to objectives, strategies, and goals—unless you tell the troops. Strategy locked in the boardroom is the worst strategy of all.

As much as I loved the booklet, it's not the only way to percolate an idea into the ranks. When Qpass (software for wireless and network operators at <www.qpass.com>) needed to bring the entire staff on board the brand wagon, it went looking for an innovative way to spread the word. It hired Methodologie, a Seattle design firm, to create a series of 30 Qpass trading cards around which they built a contest. Collect all 30 and you could win four box seats to a Mariners game and other cool prizes.

On one side each card had a visual metaphor related to the brand, and the other side held an engaging text message. All were designed to engage the players and make them brand literate while caught up in the fun of trading.

> **T** h i n k i n g **P** o i n t
>
> *Important messages like mission, vision, and values deserve*
> *innovative communication. What could you do?*

Time to Make the Donuts

They're "Off to a Great Start!" at Allied Domecq Quick Service Restaurants (the parent company of Dunkin' Donuts, Baskin-Robbins, and Togo's), where they claim to have one of the more innovative, informative, and fun orientation programs around. I'll be blunt. When I first heard about "Off to a Great Start!" I couldn't see any reason for an employee to be excited other than having three and a half days away from real work. I was suspicious because smart operators like this wouldn't invest so much time and effort simply to be trendy. Still, the thought of an endless parade of department presentations delivered via "PowerPointless" was a major yawn until they told me about QER. In donut language, that means Quick Emotional Reward.

Fans of the brand think of a visit to any of the three concepts as a Quick Emotional Reward. It is this idea of reward that creates a strong emotional engagement with the brand. The challenge was how to teach this idea of QER to new employees. Off to a Great Start was created in 2000 as the result of an employee request coupled with the realization that employees didn't seem to know enough about the brands they were hired to support.

The highlight of the program is called Business Literacy, although in practice it is given the much jazzier title of Jump Aboard the QER Express! The program covers the history of the brands; discusses the corporate mission, vision, and values; and defines the consumer. Employees are taught about franchising, how the company makes money, and the future of the industry. Imagine that! A course on how the company makes money and how you fit into the equation!

But the best part is the hands-on feature that takes the participants to Dunkin' Donuts University for a crash course on brewing Dunkin' Donuts signature coffee and a minilesson in donut finishing. (Chomp!) Then it's off to Baskin-Robbins Scoop School, where the participants are surprised to learn that style and technique really count! (When I do it, it's a simple "one scoop for me, one scoop for you"!)

In the end participants gain five pounds, an emotional connection to the product, and tremendous ownership of the brand. One participant summed it up in three magic words, "I was wowed!" Me too! Turnover that was initially 21 percent instantly dropped to 10 percent and is now under 5 percent. Does a power orientation pay? You make the call!

Tiger Training

Tiger Home Inspection, the Northeast's largest independent home inspection firm, takes every new employee on an actual home inspection as part of a new hire's orientation. From day one, even officebound employees understand from firsthand experience what is involved in a Tiger home inspection. Imagine what such an experience does for customer service representatives who handle the phones!

HOCUS, FOCUS

The lack of focus is a major cause of poor performance. And employee focus starts all the way back at the mission statement. We talk much about the corporate mission, but few employees can articulate that mission. Fewer still can tell you how what they do fits with the mission of the organization. You don't believe me? What is your corporate mission and how does what you do contribute? See? I told you so.

Good mission statements are short and in your face, mention the values, and are owned by the troops. Let's review the qualities of a good mission statement.

Short. If a mission statement is too long or cumbersome for the average person to remember, it's ineffective.

In your face. Mission statements are living documents intended to guide daily operations and decision making. It's better to reduce the mission statement to a slogan and risk being trite than to risk being irrelevant. Effective mission statements are incorporated into daily corporate life.

Mention the values. Great mission statements are value based. If your company is founded on truth, justice, and the American way, then be proud of those values and mention them in the mission statement when possible and at every instance when appropriate.

Owned by the troops. It is impossible to merely "install" a corporate culture; and hiring a consultant to create and implement a corporate culture is a waste of time. Everything is culture. The sign out front, the shrubs in the landscape, the way the phone is answered, and even the condition of the employee lounge and restrooms are culture. How the boss dresses, greets the receptionist, and handles e-mail from the front line are bigger expressions and influences of and on culture than any slogan or kickoff event will ever be.

Mission, vision, values, and even the marketing slogan must all be congruent with the corporate culture, because, in aggregate, they *are* the corporate culture.

> ### T *h i n k i n g* P *o i n t*
>
> *Are your daily operations congruent with your mission,*
> *vision, values, and brand statements?*

COACHING

"Never wrestle with a pig. You get dirty and the pig loves it."

I received a request for advice on handling conflict within a team. The e-mail came from a manager living on the other side of the world in Bangladesh, who closed by asking, "How can we save this team without having to start over?"

Conflict is an expression of stress, and stress is most often a matter of poor fit. Poor fit can come in four forms: (1) skills, (2) focus, (3) motivators, and (4) personalities. Skills can be acquired; focus can be restored; motivators can be aligned; and personalities can be fixed . . . but not legally!

Stress, when focused, can actually be beneficial. Stress of the kind that stems from having a common but difficult-to-reach goal often works to coalesce the team and frequently results in performance that is considerably better than average.

One hot summer afternoon I responded to the gruesome scene of a major automobile accident that required firefighters to use the "jaws of life" to peel back the top of a small pickup truck while I worked to help the teenage girl trapped inside. I climbed in through the passenger's side window and started to work before the paramedics arrived. A new paramedic, with whom I had never worked, climbed in through the driver's side window, and we went from total strangers to team players in a heartbeat.

I remember giving a quick report and continuing to hold the patient's spinal alignment. For some reason I don't recall, we could not immediately apply a stabilizing collar. Up one side of her sleeve he went with the bandage scissors and then, without a spoken word, we traded duties. The shears were passed to me and down the other side I went. Common training and a clear-cut goal seasoned by the stress of the moment and two guys, who would probably do little more than nod if passing at the grocery store, became an instant team.

The problem of management is to discover the source of the stress and then decide if it is good (beneficial) stress or bad stress. Attempting to remedy the wrong cause of stress may exacerbate rather than cure the problem. And eliminating good stress may do little more than lower productivity.

(The boss should be the source of all your stress!)

> **T** h i n k i n g   **P** o i n t
>
> *Is your team under enough stress?*

DECISIONS, DECISIONS

When a team player is not performing to standards, begin by asking this simple question: Could he or she perform to standard if forced? If the answer is no, you are dealing with a problem of skills. Training is in order.

If the employee could perform to standards but for whatever reason does not, training is of no value. Training an employee who can do the job but chooses not to is a matter of wrestling with a pig—all you get is dirty and the pig loves it.

The first order of training is to decide if the problem is worth solving. Too many resources are wasted on nonissues.

"How fast do you keyboard?" "One hundred twenty words per minute with one error."

Leave it alone!

The second order of business is to decide if the problem is a deficiency of knowledge. An employee who can do the work but chooses not to is not in need of training. This employee needs feedback, consequences, the removal of obstacles, or the removal of punishment. What if, in fact, you *are* dealing with a lack of knowledge? Then, and only then, is training likely to matter.

A third option exists when poor performance stems from neither a lack of motivation nor a lack of information. Sometimes you have to be honest with yourself and the employee and admit there just isn't a good fit between the talents of the employee and the talents required by the job.

If a poorly motivated employee fails to respond to feedback, consequences, and the removal of obstacles and punishment, fire the employee! You've done all that you can do. If a poorly trained employee fails to respond to training, check your original diagnosis. It may have been a matter of motivation after all. But if you were right in the first place and performance fails to improve in spite of adequate training, fire the employee. And, finally, if the matter is simply a matter of "he ain't got it," then do the humane thing—release the employee! Life doesn't always work the way we would like it to work. Rather than flogging employees who don't fit the job, why not give them the push they need to go somewhere they can be successful?

One of the major reasons for employee turnover is stress from poor performance. Yes, poor performance causes on-the-job stress. Do you really believe people enjoy going to work and failing? Not even! No one ever wakes in the morning and says, "I can't wait to go to work and look like an idiot."

The biggest training mistake is reserving training only for the purpose of fixing problems. Training is most effective when it is used to improve on strengths. Think back on the terminations you have participated in or know of. How many of those were the results of the performer not having the skills to do the job? You can't think of many, can you? As a matter of fact, I bet you can't think of a single instance when an employee was dismissed because of lack of skills. Most job failures have little or nothing with lack of skills. *Most failures are a matter of poor fit.*

Jim Collins, writing in *Good to Great,* likens a job to a bus. Collins says "the truly great companies are those that have the right person on the bus in the right seat driven by the right driver." If your bus isn't heading in the right direction at the posted speed, better stop the bus, find out if you have the right people on the bus, and if all those people are in their assigned seats. If everything checks out in the back, better take a good look in the rearview mirror.

BEHAVIOR MODIFICATION

"Spiffs," rewards, bonuses—it doesn't matter what you call them. They are nothing more than attempts to shape employee behavior, and most are wrapped around a contest. You could even say that contests are nothing more than corporate attempts at behavior modification. But if you understand how contests and games work, you have a clear picture of the larger issues of running a work team. Behavior modification is, by the way, perfectly ethical, moral, and legal when you do it right. One word that substitutes nicely for behavior modification is . . . *management!*

But back to the idea of contests. Contests that work are usually constructed to modify short-term behavior, whereas pay plans (another form of contest) and policies are focused on long-term behavior or performance. With either you must be concerned over possible unintended consequences.

One fast-food restaurant operator watched sales per transaction drop after a timer was installed to measure speed of service. Faced with an ever-ticking clock, employees abandoned attempts to sell side items and drinks in an effort to satisfy service-time standards.

Another instance shows that an auto accessories shop rewarded the sales staff for gross sales and sweetened the pot with frequent spiffs paid for units sold. The sales crew had some latitude when pricing a deal and also had those spiffs hanging temptingly close. Should anyone be surprised that the result was unnecessary discounting?

One danger of allowing performance to shape policies and systems is that inevitably when you focus on one area of performance, something else is going to suffer. Tipped employees don't want to leave the sales floor to do side work; sales persons don't want to do administrative work or customer service follow-up.

> **T** h i n k i n g **P** o i n t
>
> *The physics of contests are simple: For every motivation*
> *there is an equal and opposite motivation.*

Here's what you have to know for a contest to work: The contest term must be appropriate for the maturity of those involved; the reward must be perceived as such; the score must always be visible (and the players should keep their own score); the desired behavior must be precisely targeted; the results must be achievable; the reward should go to the team rather than an individual; and the contest must be emotionally engaging.

Maturity. If there is a single biggest flaw with performance-shaping programs, it is that too many don't take into account the emotional maturity of the players. Some folks have trouble thinking beyond Friday. A contest involving these folks that rewards performance measured over the next year is totally useless. It's better to adjust the rewards and the term.

Reward.   Win the contest and you get to go to dinner with the boss. Is that a reward or the booby prize? Well, it depends. For some folks, dinner with the boss could be a huge motivator; for others, it might be a source of embarrassment or discomfort. The best contests allow the winner to choose the reward.

Visible score.   Keeping score can be motivating. In games and other forms of contests, always knowing the score is a motivator. And it's much better to let the players keep track of their own score.

When we ran our small restaurant, we would occasionally place a tube of large drink cups in front of each register and clip a five-dollar bill to the order board. "Whoever sells their tube of large cups first can take the five bucks." Short term, everybody can relate to a five-dollar bill, and there was constant feedback in the form of two rapidly diminishing tubes of cups.

Targeted behavior.   Because of the law of motivation, which is "for every motivator there is an equal and opposite motivator," you must be careful to target the desired behavior. For an employee to sell a large drink in the case mentioned above, a customer's motivation might have been to purchase a medium drink or no drink at all. However, had we clipped a hundred-dollar bill to the order board, we bet the motivation to pick up the prize might have transcended the need to be courteous.

Achievable.   Motivate an employee against an obstacle that is insurmountable and you don't get performance; you get frustration. Ask an employee to perform a complicated task without proper tools or adequate training, and all you'll get is stress with no results. Offer a reward for performance that is unachievable, and instead of performance you'll get anger and resentment.

Too many managers make good on only a portion of the manager's credo:

> *Assemble the team.*
> *Sell the dream.*
> *Remove obstacles.*
> *Say thank you.*

Motivating a team to tackle insurmountable obstacles is worse than counterproductive, it's cruel.

Reward the team. It is usually a mistake to create a contest (performance management system) that rewards a single winner. When players enter a contest on unequal footing that relies on individual talent and experience, the other players may simply give up if early in the game a single player takes a huge lead. They may even act to sabotage the leader.

One rarely considered negative of rewarding a single player is that leaders will be motivated not to share their expertise with other team players, who might knock them from the lead.

Emotional engagement. Effective performance management systems play off what motivates the employee, not what motivates the boss. But it seems the employees aren't motivated! Yes, they are! They just aren't motivated to do what you, the boss, want them to do.

Thank God for Denny's! Without Denny's and a sure hand on an egg pan, I would never have paid my way through college. And I wouldn't understand how conflicting motivators can influence performance.

In the summer I usually worked the breakfast shift. I loved it and always thought I was pretty good at it. But when classes resumed for the fall, I switched to swing shift, working from three in the afternoon until eleven at night. I liked that too but was a bit miffed one season when the boss scheduled me to work solo every Monday, Tuesday, and Wednesday.

"Boss, how come you have me working alone all the time? Couldn't I at least get the occasional weekend breakfast shift?"

"Sorry, I need you those shifts. You're the only cook I have who can work those shifts by himself. If I schedule someone else, I'll have to add a second body to handle the rush. You're the fast one."

"We can fix that!" It was a threat that earned me a favored Saturday breakfast run.

Years later I had a great kid working for me in my fast-food restaurant. He was fast, clean, and personable—everything you could ask for in an employee of any age. At least until he met Krista. All of a sudden the kid who was always early to report could barely make it to work on time. Most bosses would say that he had lost his motivation, but that would be totally wrong. This kid was, and continued to be, highly motivated. The problem was that the motivator had changed. Suddenly,

FIGURE 12.1   *Employee's Motivators*

Employee Rank	What Employees Want	Boss's Rank
	Interesting work	
	Recognition for a job well done	
	Being in the know	
	Job security	
	Good wages	
	Opportunity for promotion	
	Good working conditions	
	Friends at work	
	Fair treatment and discipline	
	Help with personal problems	

instead of being turned on by the kudos earned for good performance at work, he was turned on by a sweet young thing named Krista.

> **T** *h i n k i n g*   **P** *o i n t*
>
> *The boss has to find out exactly what it is that motivates*
> *each individual employee and figure out how*
> *to turn that to an advantage.*

As part of your regular performance reviews, make sure to ask employees to list what they want from their work experience and ask them to grade the company on its delivery. See Figure 12.1.

Don't cheat! Rank the items from 1 to 10 from the perspective of the boss. We'll get back to this.

If you want to discover what actually motivates your employees, ask them individually. Ask them to make a list of what is important to them in a work relationship. Ask for the list in order of importance followed by a grade on your ability to deliver. You'll get results that look something like the two samples in Figure 12.2.

The charts in Figures 12.1 and 12.2 show that a one-size-fits-all performance management system isn't the way to get the most from a team. So back to the chart, What Employees Want. The items are already listed

FIGURE 12.2 *Joe's and Margaret's Motivators*

Joe's Motivators	Grade
Good pay	A
Opportunity to network with industry peers	C
Benefits	B
Annual training seminars	C
Always knowing where I stand	A

Marcia's Motivators	Grade
Freedom to attend family events	A
No age discrimination	A
Car allowance	A
Insurance	C
Opportunity to work independently	A

in typical employee ranking! Notice that good pay falls near the middle of the range as ranked by employees. We bet you ranked it somewhere near the top!

"So what" is exactly what many employees say when they hear about the latest contest or pay plan. Just as customers define what great service is, employees define what's good for them; and you aren't going to know how to motivate your crew unless you ask.

> **T** h i n k i n g **P** o i n t
>
> *How could you discover what "turns on" each of your employees, and could you devise a reward system that caters to each individual personality?*

13

REMOVING OBSTACLES

"I'd like the chicken fried steak with mashed potatoes instead of the fries, please." That was my mother speaking, happy to save me a few cents by ordering the senior special. "I'm sorry. The chicken special only comes with fries." It was clear the server had had this conversation before. I interrupted, saying, "Ma'am, I don't mind paying extra." "I'm sorry. The boss is pretty firm about no substitutions." "Okay, I don't want to put you on the spot. Do this. Sell us an order of mashed potatoes and leave the fries off the chicken fried steak. How's that?"

It seemed that arguing for a commonsense solution wouldn't be worth the effort. So I'll just buy an extra order of mashed potatoes. How much could that be? Apparently priceless. "I'm sorry; we can't sell a side of mashed potatoes. They're only available on the fried chicken dinner." "Fine. Bring my mom the chicken fried steak. I'll have the fried chicken dinner. Please put the potatoes for both orders on the side. Can you do that?"

The server was visibly relieved.

Most of what we do to aggravate customers is unintentional and often the result of simply missing the details or failing to notice unintended consequences. Surprisingly, it is more often the little things that seem meaningless when they occur singly but leave us saying, "I don't like that place," when combined. These little insults, usually too small to bubble up to the level of awareness, we call microinsults. I'll point out a few but I warn you: Once you see one microinsult, you'll start seeing them everywhere!

Microinsults

- Hotel communications surcharge. (An otherwise nice hotel posted this sign: "In order to upgrade our phone system, there will be a $3 communications surcharge added to your bill.")
- Hotel TV cabinets that don't stay open
- "'Scuse the cart" announcements in airports
- Hotel shampoo containers with tops that won't close
- Taxis that smell like an ashtray
- Nonworking automatic spigots at Chicago O'Hare Airport restrooms
- CNN Airport Network whose volumes are too low to be heard
- Restaurants with smoking sections in the front of the dining area
- Too many clothes racks in a store to shop comfortably
- Paying at the gasoline pump, where you are asked how you will pay, if you want a car wash, and if you want a receipt—if you like to be interrogated by a machine!
- Prepackaged produce that forces you to buy three tomatoes no matter what!
- Double doors, but one, the one you tried first, is locked
- More than a two-day wait for anything—mower repair, car repair, and so on.
- Toll-free number for ordering but not for problem resolution
- Being asked "Smoking or non?"
- Bed linens in hotels tucked together and forcing you to remake the bed
- Hotel desk chairs that are too short for the desk
- Meridian hotel voice mail: "To confirm that, you want to delete..."
- POP (point of purchase) materials in hotel rooms

It's the System

Dr. W. Edwards Deming, the guru of Total Quality Management (TQM), was not known as a customer service leader, but he was. Deming understood that the customer, not corporate convenience, should be the focus of systems for delivering products and services. "The consumer," said Deming "is the most important part of the production line."

He also insists that workers work within a system that, try as they might, is beyond their control. It is the system, not their individual skills, that determines how they perform. And only management can change the system.

In simpler language, it's not the stupid worker. It's the stupid work.

Iced

Not all obstacles to a job well done can be seen with the naked eye because not all are physical. Some are fiscal. A client in the supermarket industry tells of the time he walked into one of his chain's stores and was nearly run over by a tiny woman wheeling a giant barrel of ice through the produce department. He recognized her as the manager of the seafood department.

"Regina, what's with the ice?" "Our machine is broken so I have to bootleg from produce." The small woman was barely visible from behind the barrel.

"How long before it's fixed?" "Who knows? It's been over a month." She continued to shove the big yellow barrel around the bananas, then skittered to the right to avoid a display of kiwi. "What's worse is that I spend so much time playing traveling ice machine that you can actually notice a drop in department sales. I have to actually be there, behind the counter, if you want me to be serious about selling seafood!"

"I get your point. Are the parts on back order?" The view had shifted to her backside as she pressed on, head bowed, and shoulder pressed against the cold plastic. "Budget" was her parting word.

From the produce department, he went up the steps to the manager's office. "I was just about flattened by Regina. She's pretty disgusted." My friend offered an opening through which you could easily drive a conversation. "Oh, you mean the Ice Queen." "No, I meant Regina. Seriously, she sounded pretty unhappy. What's with the ice machine?"

"What did she tell you?" "Budget, but that can't be right." "It's right. We're behind on profits and we've been told not to spend a dime. So I haven't."

In an instant my client scooped up all the pens and pencils he could find lying on the desktop and placed them into the top desk drawer. Then he ripped the drawer from the desk and headed downstairs.

"Hey! Where are you going with my stuff? I've got work to do!"

"So long as Regina's ice machine is on the fritz, you can find your pencils in the produce department."

The machine was up and running in a matter of hours.

Valuing System over Satisfaction

My brother Stuart attempted to return a wedding gift that had been purchased locally and was a duplicate. He wanted to exchange the gift for another of equal value, which in most places would be the proverbial no-brainer.

When he approached the clerk, he was told there could be no exchanges without a sales receipt. "This was a wedding gift and we don't have a receipt." "How do we know that this isn't merchandise stolen from us that you are attempting to return?" "We can give you the name of the person who purchased the gift. You can easily check her account to verify that she purchased it here." Now Stu is not known for either great patience or excessive tact. By this time, his temperature had to be beyond boiling! "Look, you could have found out what this lady purchased, stolen something identical, and now be attempting to return it. We have to have strict policies to protect ourselves. That's just good business. Sorry."

Yep. Sorry says it all.

WHAT TO DO?

Is it possible that you, too, have in at least a small way created a system that puts the customer second?

Our restaurant was located within a few hundred yards of the site of the annual Fourth of July fireworks display. Nearly everyone in our little town as well as the populations of half a dozen surrounding small towns would turn out for the big event.

The show started at "dark-thirty" on the fourth. If you didn't arrive at least two hours early, your chances of a reasonable parking space were somewhere between slim and none. By the time the first blast shook the building and drew a collective "Oooohhhh!" from the waiting crowd, our parking lot was gridlocked. The drive-through self-imploded and was useful for little more than walk-up traffic, which was considerable.

The most popular service we offered was the restroom. About 30 minutes after our first surge of large drink orders, the line began to form. Through the dining room, out the door, and into the parking lot the line of the needy snaked impatiently.

One Fourth of July, a new employee, who had been assigned to keep the dining room looking good, rushed into the kitchen to report, "We'd better do something! There are tons of people in line to use our restroom, and they aren't all customers! What should I do?"

What do you think was the answer? "Tell them that restrooms are for guests only?" No! "Make sure that there is plenty of TP and that the place is immaculate. And while you're at it, take them some courtesy drinks and a few samples of chicken tenders!"

> **T** h i n k i n g   **P** o i n t
>
> *What can you do to make sure that customers*
> *are more important than systems?*

Walk through your business as though you were a customer. Start with your Yellow Pages ad. Have you made it easy for your customers to know where you are, what you do, and why you are different from the competition? Is there anything in your ad to hint that customers are not first, such as limited hours of operation?

Call your place of business. Is the phone answered by a computer or a person? Is it easy to get to the people who can solve a customer's problem?

Are your people playing big shot and leaving their phone on voice mail all day, or do they answer their phone personally within a ring or two? Do they pick up the receiver or immediately push the speakerphone button?

Is the product easy to touch, try on, or try out? Are salespeople easy to find and friendly once found? Do you offer a variety of methods of payment? Do you have to wait in line? Is there enough staff on duty to serve customers quickly?

> **T** h i n k i n g   **P** o i n t
>
> *How could you make it easy to do business with you?*

I'll Have the Usual

At the Burger Barn you are going to get hugged, at least if Vicki is there. If Kat is on duty, you'll get a hug but of a different kind.

"Kat, what are the odds that you're going to refill my iced tea before I choke on this burger?"

"I don't know. What are the odds that it's snowing in hell? What's the matter? Did you wake up grouchy?"

"No, I let her sleep. Now bring me some tea before I die of thirst!"

"Get it yourself or be nice to me. Take your choice!"

Camille Keith, Goddess of Special Marketing at Southwest Airlines (I have given her a promotion!), was telling me that one reason service can be so awful is that the person on the other side of the counter isn't likely to be around next year, maybe not even next month or next week.

What she meant to say is that servers who don't expect to see you again may not be so careful when it comes to protecting the relationship. It becomes acceptable for them to make their bad day your bad day. And this, among other reasons, is why it is important to work on retaining great customer servers.

Camille doesn't live in Center Point, Texas. In small towns, in addition to big city amenities like traffic and limited parking, we're short on a key essential for poor service—anonymity. When customers and servers are anonymous, service stinks. One key measure for ensuring good customer service is to deny anonymity.

Kat isn't going to give me bad service any day, if for no other reason than she knows she is going to see me again. If I eat at the Burger Barn (and there aren't many choices in Center Point), I'm going to sit in her station. (There's only one!) So besides being a naturally nice person, Kat's going to give me great service because she knows she is going to see me again . . . at the grocery, the MiniMart, and, of course, sitting at the Burger Barn wondering if someone woke up Grouchy.

Name Tags

The reason too many companies pin a big, bold name tag on their employees is not to help you establish a relationship. No, that tag is so you can pin on a bit of guilt should an employee not give you a receipt, treat you rudely, or otherwise break a corporate commandment, which is precisely how name tags should *not* be used.

We were dining in St. Louis, and I was about a quart low on water. No problem. Pouring water at the next table was a server whose name tag read David in big block letters.

"Excuse me, David." He poured next door but never looked up.

"David?" Still no sign of life.

"Yo! Dave!" Nothing. I was thinking that perhaps he was hearing impaired, so I tapped him on the arm as he passed. I looked him straight in the eye in case he was capable of reading lips. He turned, looked at me, and in my best read-my-lips diction I said, "David, would you mind topping off my water?" I pronounced it "waaaa tur" to be certain of the read.

He looked at me as though I were out of my mind. Then a small light flickered just behind his eyes as he grabbed for the name tag on his shirt and said, "I'm Ralph. Don't pay any attention to these things. We're required to wear them, and I just borrowed this one. Mine's at home."

Name tags work when bosses are positive and intend to catch and reward team players for doing something right.

Name tags also work for customers who use them to establish the service relationship that we define as a "personal relationship that only lasts a moment." When you're a customer, don't be shy about calling the server by name. Treat the customer-server relationship as you would any polite relationship.

"Hello, Sal! My name is Scott. Have you got time to help me pick out a new chainsaw?"

On the happy side, name tags are designed to facilitate the rapid establishment of that momentary personal relationship that we call customer service.

On the ugly but practical side, name tags are useful because they deny anonymity. "I know you and now you know that I know you."

Regular Joe

Think for a moment about why folks gravitate toward Starbucks. It could be the coffee, but I suspect that coffee is only part of the reason. At Starbucks there is a certain feeling of belonging, an attitude of "I appreciate designer coffee, and these other folks do too." Starbucks is more a clubhouse than a coffeehouse.

We see this same camaraderie at Einstein's Bagels, one of our favorite Las Vegas morning stops. At Einstein's, folks are likely to be reading the paper, and they are also likely to lean toward your table and ask, "Could I see that section if you are finished with it?"

They know it's okay to ask because we're all in the same "let's eat healthy and start our day in a mellow way" club.

A little place on Washington Boulevard in Venice Beach brings out the same feeling. Actually, you can find places everywhere where conversation is encouraged and it's just fine to share a table. At the OST Café in Bandera, Texas, perfect strangers sit together at long tables made of slabs of cypress. (It must be okay as a faded sign inside the door says, "Howdy! Seat yerself and share the tables!")

What is the lesson? Actually, there are three!

Lesson one: If you are a customer, become a regular. Help the servers get to know you as a person. If this is a one-shot transaction, do whatever it takes to let the server know you recognize her as a human being. Help a server see you in human terms. As a quick example, I would never begin a complaint by simply stating the problem. Always approach servers first in human terms: "Don't you just hate it when your reservations get messed up?"

"I'll bet you're tired of hearing this . . . "

Lesson two: If you are a server, take a moment to get to know your customers. This may take but a fraction of a second, but it's worth the effort because it's more fun working with people than numbers. "Where are you guys from?" "Do you live in the neighborhood?" "Is this a special occasion?"

Lesson three: If you are the boss (Warning! This is going to be counterintuitive), do whatever it takes to make your business seem smaller than it really is. Even if you run a huge store, you can make an effort to schedule the same cashier for the number one register on weekdays. Let each department develop its own personality. Put faces on your people so that your customers can get to know them. Why do you think there is a greeter at Wal-Mart?

We see companies putting employee pictures on the Internet so that disconnected telephone voices will seem warmer and more approachable. Do whatever you can to turn your business into a small-town business, a place of good cheer where everybody knows your name!

WHEN EMPLOYEES DON'T WANT TO PLAY

We were all set to work with our client and his team on the concept of Positively Outrageous Service. It was to be a big deal, the kind of razzle-dazzle introduction that would have the whole place buzzing with ideas for delivering Positively Outrageous Service and dreaming great dreams about innovative marketing events.

I made the big mistake of suggesting that, before I would arrive, the employees should be surveyed to see if they had a few good ideas for making customers say, Wow! At least, it seemed like a good idea.

When my client asked the employees for ideas for wowing the customers, the response was a bit less than overwhelming. It turned out that the employees felt that simple, expected actions such as smiling and offering customers a friendly greeting should be enough to pass as Positively Outrageous Service.

Sorry, folks, but our surveys show that consistently good service is no longer enough to earn a place in the hearts of your customers. Today, consistently good service doesn't win any prizes. In fact, consistently good service is the minimum ticket to get into the game.

When we randomly surveyed 600 Americans and asked how the service at full-service retailers compared with that of the big-box discounters, we were shocked. Sixty-two percent of our survey group said that full-service retailers provide service that is either very good or excellent. That's not bad unless you look at the score for the big-box discounters. They managed to con 64 percent of consumers into rating their service as either very good or excellent.

What does that mean? It means that the horror stories you've heard about service at the big-box discount stores are only part of the picture. Your friends have been telling you the bad things just to make you feel better. Well, those same friends told us an entirely different story. What you want to know is what to do about it.

First, employees are not psychic. What seems elementary, obvious, or plain old common sense isn't when it comes to serving customers, at least not to employees. This means that if you really expect good service, even Positively Outrageous Service, you've got to tell your employees what it is.

Second (and get this because it's important), you can't decree great service. You have to demonstrate it and reward it. Demonstrating great service is nothing more than simple leadership. Take everything you've heard about learning theory and forget it except for this: People learn by doing. The things that people are likely to do are things that they see in their environment and can imitate. That makes you, the boss and their leader, the only true training program. Whatever you do, the team will imitate.

If you run to the office when the floor gets busy, why should you be surprised when employees retreat to the stockroom rather than deal with a bunch of messy customers? On the other hand, if you make it a habit to seek out customers and go the extra mile to serve them well, guess what will happen darned near automatically?

A friend of mine, a bank president, decided to move his desk into the open area immediately inside the bank's front door so that if you are in the bank, you are in his office. Got any ideas how the employees in this bank treat customers? Would you consider moving your office onto the sales floor? Would you do it? Go ahead. I dare you!

Beyond a great example, there must be real training, the kind of how-to training that provides employees with concrete suggestions for dealing with customers and specific techniques for selling and providing service. If your employees could figure this out for themselves, you'd be working for them!

Finally, there has to be a reward system designed to reinforce great customer service. For many employees, the fact that they are able to help someone solve a problem is sufficient reward. It's too bad that in the real world, this won't be true for every employee. Most humans can't avoid evaluating their efforts in terms of what's in it for them.

In the old days, if you did a good job, you got to keep it. These aren't the good old days. Today, suggesting that good work earns you the right to stay doesn't cut it. This is especially true for the better employees, who can get self-satisfaction and monetary compensation to go along with it someplace else.

It's too easy to say, "You can't get good help any more." You *can* get good help. You can find honest, dependable, motivated employees. Once you find the raw talent, it's up to you to turn that talent into superstars with examples, training, and rewards.

Simple? Yes.

Easy? No.

But then, if it were easy, everybody would be in the business!

SHOW ME THE MONEY

"We're a people company" is a phrase that shows up all too often and means all too little. It's easy to say and is usually heartfelt but rarely true. There are, however, exceptions. Find yourself ten feet in the door of The Container Store (there are some 20 around the country) and unless you just moved here from Mars, you will instantly know something isn't quite right. Actually, the uneasy feeling comes from things being almost too right.

The first employee you encounter—and it will be sooner rather than later—will give you a Ritz-Carlton greeting that often out-Ritzes the Ritz. Okay, that could be a fluke. By the time you have met your third or fourth employee (and each one outshines the other), you will suspect that you've died and gone to service Heaven.

While you are looking at containers for mailing CDs or boxes for storing sweaters under your bed, you might notice that the retail clerks look, act, and speak like regular people, people you might know or would trust to visit your home.

Something's right and that something is The Container Store's dedication to actually practicing "We're a people company" mantra.

If *Fast Company* has it right, the average retail clerk gets a whopping seven hours of training, a figure that, based on the service delivered, seems unimaginably high. The Container Store people log in an incredible 235 hours of training their first year. That's about 200 hours more than the average retail clerk lasts on the job!

Does training pay? The company consistently posts double-digit annual sales growth. 'Nuf said? Training isn't cheap, but it *is* a bargain. Two managers were debating the cost-benefit ratio of training dollars. The first manager said, "What if we spend a pile of dollars and they decide to leave?" "Yeah, but what if we don't train them and they decide to stay?"

14

WHAT MAKES WORK WORTHWHILE

Boss spelled backwards, according to some, is double SOB. Check out the weekly surveys on Monster.com, and if you live in the executive suite, it may be time to put duct tape and plastic on the windows.

One recent Monster survey asked, "When was the last time your boss said, 'Well done'?" Thirty-three percent said—never! Twelve percent said—last year! (The judges rule that last year and never are psychological equivalents.) Check it out, Dude. The workplace just isn't getting stroked! It's no wonder that motivational speakers are making all the dough!

And here's a surprise. The Monster.com people wanted to know if employees considered themselves loyal to the company. Do you want to guess? How about these two delightful responses? Thirty-nine percent said, "I'm loyal to the highest bidder." (This one actually makes sense because based on Enron, WorldCom, and others, the bosses feel the same way!) Sixteen percent said, "No, I'm only trying to gain experience."

The two categories combine for the sole purpose of making the remaining 43 percent feel stupid.

Asked what they would most like to say to their boss, 46 percent would use but two lovely words: "I quit." A whopping 26 percent of an obviously insecure workforce thinks, "I could be the next to go."

How about a round of applause for job security and company loyalty? You may as well go ahead and turn them loose! Asked what would make them happiest, 36 percent say, "Figuring out which career is right for me!"

And, finally, when asked, "What are you most thankful for at work," did the crowd reply with "I'm part of a great team!" or perhaps "The chance to learn new things"? Nope. It was simply, "That I still have a job."

THE BEST JOB IS . . .

According to the *Jobs Rated Almanac,* the best job in America is— drum roll, please—*a financial planner!* Web site manager and computer systems analyst follow in positions two and three. Be still my heart! Tied for fourth were computer programmer and actuary.

Who's at the bottom? How about an ironworker, cowboy, and lumberjack? And don't forget a fisherman and an oil field roustabout! Only the president of the United States edged out a firefighter for the worst working environment.

Well, here's the deal. The *Jobs Rated Almanac* doesn't determine what is the best or the worst job for *you.* You make that decision.

This morning we responded to a very ugly EMS call. The scene was too gross to describe, so sickening that at one point a sheriff's deputy said to me, "You'd better get inside. The new medic is losing it!" So I jumped the porch rail, bounded through the living room, and said to a very pale medic, "I've got it! Take a break!"

But if you'd call Station Three this instant and ask the medic if he would like to hang up his bandage shears and become an actuary, see what he says. My money is on "No way!"

> ### T h i n k i n g   P o i n t
>
> *Work won't ever be good unless the rest of your life is good.*

Start by promising yourself that you actually have the rest of your life! If you find yourself thinking there's no time to get a life, then it's time to realize that having a life can actually help your career.

If you're a boss, you had better make darned good and sure that your team has a life on the other side of the office door. Otherwise, you can count on two things: they aren't giving their best, and they aren't likely to be long-term employees. Workaholics are rarely business successes, but they are always family failures.

Manage your personal life as you would manage a business. Make personal decisions as if they were profit or loss decisions. One of the first decisions you must make is whether you can sustain the way you are working today for a decade or longer. If the answer is no, it's time to start thinking about an exit strategy.

AW SHUCKS, I HAVE TO GO TO . . .

If you finish this sentence, "Aw shucks, I have to go to . . . play," aren't you the odd duck! But ask people who are doing what they really want to do, and you'll discover that they often have great difficulty drawing a line between work and play. The nine-to-five crowd dismisses them as hopelessly type A, but the few of us who really have this work thing dialed in understand that when you are doing what you love, you love what you're doing.

What exactly is the difference between work and play? It's up to you to define.

Charles Coonradt, a friend of mine who wrote *The Game of Work* (Game of Work, 1997), says several things are universal when it comes to games. Games have a clearly defined objective, a readily visible score, and are usually played with kids you like. Work, says Coonradt, should be more like a game and then you might be inclined to say, "Hey everybody! I get to go to work!"

Here are a few ideas for making work more like play:

- *Decide if you are in a job you love.* Sometimes the best way to make your job fun is to get another one!
- *Be competent.* If you want the freedom to play the game your way, it helps to be a competent player. Bosses hate surprises, and it's a known fact that nervous bosses aren't fun.
- *Play appropriately.* If you don't know when to be serious, the boss won't tolerate much that isn't squarely inside the box.
- *Build a team of winners.* It's no fun to play on a losing team.
- *Choose fun names that clearly identify people and things* in terms of what they really do. Maybe the boss could become Coach and the maintenance guy Official Cleaner Upper! Do this for processes, products, and policies. Southwest Airlines has a People Department!

- *Schedule time for play.* Dream up reasons to celebrate, and while you are at it, party smart. All the time isn't the right time for play.
- *Learn the cues and clues* that let you know when customers and others are in the mood to play.
- *Keep score.* Make sure that players keep their own score, that the score is always visible, and that team performance, in addition to individual performance, is rewarded.
- *Sign your work.* You won't believe how important this is. People love to show off and connect what they do with results in the real world. Anything you can do to connect workers with customers improves quality and gives work meaning.
- *Introduce complexity.* We've gone too far to dummy down jobs. Add complexity, and productivity will go up, not down.
- *Start the day with a briefing.* The best way to get everyone on the same page is to start each shift with a short briefing.

Best Job

I first encountered the *Jobs Rated Almanac* through an article in the newspaper during a time when I had been working with a wonderful crew of wildland firefighters, and we had just returned from a fire set by some loser in the wee hours of the morning. We returned to the station smelling of smoke and sweat, still high on the moment. We returned as victorious warriors of a battle no one had seen other than ourselves.

As we gathered in the kitchen, the smell of frying bacon began to dominate and the crackle of eggs replaced the roar of burning timber. One of the firefighters picked up the paper and read an article about firefighting being one of the worst jobs you could have. A financial planner was number one, according to the article.

A freckled kid, young enough to be my son but sharp enough to earn my respect, said, "This has to have been written by someone who works in a windowless cubicle!" Margy, the tough-as-nails Renaissance woman who was our captain, smiled from behind her mug of hot coffee. Once back home, Margy and I exchanged a few e-mails. Below is her last. Notice her ending comment about her work, and ask yourself if you are so lucky:

Scott,
Honestly, I have no recollection of sending you a quote from my dad! But if I had sent one, it would have been this one, written by David Grayson (unknown date) and recorded by Dad in a worn three-ring notebook:

"Happiness, I have discovered, is nearly always a rebound from hard work. It is one of the follies of men to imagine that they can enjoy mere thought, or emotion, or sentiment. As well, try to eat beauty. For happiness must be tricked! She loves to see men at work. She loves sweat, weariness, self-sacrifice. She will be found not in palaces but lurking in cornfields and factories and hovering over littered desks: she crowns the unconscious head of the busy child. If you look up suddenly from hard work you will see her, but if you look too long she fades sorrowfully away.

"There is something fine in hard physical labor. One actually stops thinking. I often work long without any thought whatever, so far as I know, save that connection with the monotonous repetition of the labor itself—down with the spade, out with it, over with it—and repeat. And yet sometimes, mostly in the forenoon when I am not tired at all, I will suddenly have a sense of the world opening around me—a sense of its beauty and its meaning—giving me a peculiar deep happiness that is near complete content."

That's the time on the hoselay when you look at your partner with a big grin and say, "This sucks, doesn't it?" Ha, ha.

> **T h i n k i n g   P o i n t**
>
> *Is there ever a time in your work when you can grin and say, "This sucks, doesn't it? Ha, ha?"*

Good Work

While working the Borrowed Dreams project, we were surprised to discover that some jobs we wouldn't take short of pure survival were considered highly desirable to others. Working in a hotel laundry room was simply awful, yet we came away from a very short stint as an Iowa hog farmer thinking, "I could get into that!"

A Border Patrol agent was pretty cool, although working as a deckhand on an oil tanker got pretty old after a few days at sea. Being a wildland firefighter was my favorite but a medic on a helicopter ambulance was not.

But each of those jobs was loved, perhaps even coveted, by some, not all, of the regular team players. What's the point? While not everyone is on the right bus, there *is* a right bus for almost everyone. The folks in the hotel laundry room loved it. And the workers in the dark, hot, and incredibly noisy foundry at John Deere had only one regret, that it isn't likely these jobs will be around for their children and grandchildren!

Beyond the work itself, we discovered that four features make work good, or not good. These features are curiously similar to the features that make games fun. Here's our list: choice, risk, score, and purpose.

Choice

Great work has freedom of choice. Not the freedom to choose whether the work will be done but the freedom to choose how, perhaps when, and in what order it will be done.

We learned the importance of choice while chasing drug smugglers on the Mexican border. In the wild, wooly mountains east of San Diego, Border Patrol agents play a nightly game of cowboy; they are savvy modern-day gunslingers who use their brains far more frequently than their bullets to outsmart the bad guys attempting to cross our borders and our laws to deliver loads of contraband. What makes the work so darned interesting is that in the heat of the moment there is no time to consult a manual or even a supervisor. It's act now and act right, or the opportunity will melt back into the shadows.

Risk

All great work involves an element of risk. It could be financial risk, physical risk, even emotional risk, but all great work involves risk, because without risk it's hard to say "I did it!" without the obvious rejoinder, "So what?" Hog farmers, firefighters, and commissioned salespeople let it all hang out.

Score

Unless you keep score, no work is as good as it can be. Workers in the hotel laundry counted and charted sheets that were processed and towels that were handled. Even working as a carnie (carnival worker) in the hot desert air of Arizona we carefully counted tickets and riders. The best scoring systems are always visible, and the score is kept by the players, not the boss.

Purpose

Good work makes us bigger. Good work gives us purpose. For the same reason that the guy who wouldn't put a buck in the Salvation Army kettle will participate in the United Way drive at work, we all like to be part of teams and work that make us bigger than who we are.

If there is a corollary to purpose, it must be this: Art happens when worker and customer connect. When the connection between the work you do and the impact it makes on a real, live customer is strong, work becomes something more than a physical action. When worker and customer connect, you get emotional involvement and from that comes art.

After a very long shift as a pastry chef at a Doubletree Hotel, my mentor advised, "We have one more thing to do. Turn your apron clean side out and come with me." I was totally puzzled as Tony led me away from the mixers and ovens deep in the heart of the hotel to the lobby, where he posted us at near attention close to a small retail shop. On display were racks of the cookies, pies, and other pastries that we had prepared by the dozens.

"Tony, why are we standing here?" "Because the customer will see the cookies and look at you. And they will know that you are the cookie man!"

Now, I've been around the block a time or two, and, frankly, baking a couple hundred dozen cookies may be hard work, but it's really no big deal until a customer walks up to the display and begins to choose. And then I found myself thinking, "Pick the chocolate chip cookies! Those are the ones I baked!"

Art happens when worker and customer connect.

A few weeks after my pastry lesson, I found myself cooking steaks to order at the same time chicken and orange roughy were baking in the oven. We were in an all-electric kitchen rolling south at 75 miles an hour aboard Amtrak, and except for the occasional stretch of rough track, we were focused on fixing a hot dinner for the 52 passengers waiting patiently on the second level of the dining car.

It's difficult, but not impossible, to conduct an interview while cooking for a small army. I had all but exhausted my questions when I asked, "What's the worst thing about this job?" when we hit a new section of track. The ride got as smooth as a baby's bottom, and the car got quiet except for the sizzle and pop of the steaks on the griddle.

"Funny thing," said the chef, as he removed his tall white hat to think and wipe away the sweat. "The only thing that really gets me is that while we're down here cooking what I think is a pretty darned good meal, the 52 folks upstairs are wondering how Marriott managed to do such a good job of catering. They have no idea that we actually cook this stuff from scratch, and that really galls me."

"I know what to do," I said, as I reached for my apron strings. And again, art happened.

IT'S ALL ABOUT THE CUSTOMER

15

LOYALTY, ANYONE?

Satisfied customers are pleased with the moment. Loyal customers are pleased with the relationship. The most important difference between customers who are loyal and those who are merely satisfied is this: Loyal customers are resistant to change.

A satisfied customer who was pleased with you this morning may be tempted by a competitor's coupon this afternoon. In fact, you might say that satisfied customers are price sensitive, whereas loyal customers are emotionally sensitive.

Too many organizations are enamored with customer satisfaction ratings while giving short shrift to what is truly important, the depth of their customer relationships.

For us, living in the boonies, our shopping trip of 15 minutes into town takes us right past a new supermarket. It's close, it's convenient, and the prices are competitive. But when the Sunday paper gets hauled up the hill from our box on the highway, coupons from this store are immediately deposited in the recycle bin without so much as a glance. If you ask Buns why, she says, "It's not my store."

"What do you mean 'It's not my store'? It's a couple of miles closer, the parking is easier, and they carry the same brands! What if their coupon is a good deal?" This, of course, is husband logic. Wife logic over-rules: "They'll be close on price, and it's not my store."

She's a loyal customer, resistant to change. Loyalty matters on the bottom line. (Later I'll talk about how to build loyalty.)

T *h i n k i n g*   **P** *o i n t*

Are your customers (employees) loyal or merely satisfied?

Are your customers satisfied? If you answer yes, what does that mean? For years we have been preaching the gospel of Positively Outrageous Service and saying that to generate strong customer loyalty, customers must first be served and then absolutely wowed. In other words, there are degrees of satisfaction.

You can pretty much assume that if a customer doesn't lodge a complaint, she must be satisfied at least to some degree. But just how satisfied must that customer be to come back, or better yet, resist the entreaties of competition advertising?

A discovery by Xerox, reported in the *Harvard Business Review* (Nov.–Dec. 1995), showed that "totally satisfied customers" (we'd call them "wowed") were six times more likely to repurchase Xerox products over the next 18 months than were merely satisfied customers.

You *can* put a price on building loyalty through Positively Outrageous Service. Just for fun, use the six times figure calculated by Xerox (actual numbers will vary depending on driving habits) to see what it would be worth to your bottom line if you could move 10 percent of your satisfied customers all the way to wowed. For us the difference would be . . . holy smokes! I just put a pen to this and the number is huge! Go ahead! Try it for yourself!

The reason that loyalty sales are so profitable is that they incur almost zero additional marketing or administrative cost. Whatever loyalty adds to the top line falls all the way to the bottom line with the exception of the cost of goods. If the majority of your customers fall into the satisfied category, it's panic time—you're missing huge loyalty-generated opportunities.

But the mistake comes in paying too much for loyalty. Read on.

TAKE INSURANCE . . . PLEASE

A survey by the Insurance Information Institute (III)—and we're assuming this will at least partially apply to other industries—discovered that satisfied customers would have to save 20 percent before thinking that switching carriers was worth the hassle. If you think about it, 20 percent is a pretty wide margin. But the III also discovered that 15 percent of insurance customers wouldn't switch for any reason. These are the loyal customers.

What kinds of customers would you rather have: customers who could be enticed by price or customers who are darned near bullet proof? Two lessons can be learned. First, the odds are that you could increase your prices and not lose enough customers to offset the additional profits. In other words, you could serve fewer customers at a higher margin. The second lesson comes in the form of a question: What if you could substantially increase the number of your customers who are loyal rather than merely satisfied?

And the bonus round: Based on the above two thoughts, how might you change your marketing? Because some customers will always leave for price, perhaps a better strategy would be to stop chasing price-sensitive customers, raise your prices, and focus on increasing customer loyalty!

> **T** *h i n k i n g* **P** *o i n t*
>
> *What could you do to make service so good*
> *that it's worth a premium?*

And just how much is a loyal customer worth? The answer is probably as much myth as fact when it comes to the value of loyal customers. We say they cost less to serve. We imagine that loyal customers have established a bond with products or servers or even habit that motivates their willingness to pay more. And we like to believe that loyal customers are great marketers for products they love.

But none of that is unconditionally true.

Loyal customers, call them "regulars" if you will, often want and demand more, not less, service. Regulars feel entitled to special treatment precisely because they *are loyal.* The same applies to price. High-volume regular customers are acutely aware of their value to the business and often expect lower, not higher, prices.

Some years ago one of our loyal customers called me to his office, smiled, and slid a single sheet of paper across the desk. To set the stage, we were producing at the time video-based training programs for this international, multi-billion-dollar retailer. When we pitched the account, we went in with a low bid with the expectation that landing this chunk of regular business would easily crack our monthly nut and enable us to charge a bit more for smaller projects. After several years of dedicated effort, this loyal customer had *not* become cheaper to serve. The economies of scale and working on multiple projects materialized as forecast. What wasn't forecast was that the client would often change plans at the last moment, sending us into "overwhelm" when we had to make revisions and reschedule our crew. Oh, and did I mention that our competition was always breathing down our necks with its version of a "foot-in-the-door" bid? Well, it was. But not to worry; our client was loyal—just not all that profitable, and on some projects they just plain ate our lunch.

To continue . . . He pushed the paper again, expecting that I would meet him halfway and slip it from the desk. "What's this, Dave?" Dave was my buddy. Sure, I paid for lunch—every time. Sure, we often treated him and his wife to dinner. It was a business expense.

"What's this, Dave?" "Those are your new prices. My budget has been trimmed, and I'm passing along the savings." This from my "buddy," the guy who had over the previous few months begun to be rude to my crew and who frequently failed to show up for a shoot. A loyal customer. We fired him. And that next year was our most profitable ever.

In many cases loyal customers are not cheaper to serve, and they expect lower, not higher, prices in exchange for their dependable, if not all that profitable, business.

> **T** *h i n k i n g* **P** *o i n t*
>
> *Not all business is good business.*

(If you move your lips when you read, you'll look funny reading this next subtitle.)

LOYAL, LOYAL, LOYAL!

Remember, our definition of customer loyalty is resistance to change. The idea is to create the feeling of "I can't get this anywhere else but here." If you're selling a commodity item, it is difficult (but not impossible) to create loyalty. And if you intentionally turn your product or service into a commodity . . . shame on you!

Last week we had a craving for pizza, something hot and fresh, spicy and smothered in cheese, just the thing to go with a cold beer and middle-age spread. So we stopped at a place where we knew we could get the cure.

"Buns, I can't go in there."

"Why not? It's just a pizza. Eating a pizza once in a blue moon isn't going to kill you."

"That's not the problem. I don't have a coupon. They'll laugh at me if I don't have a coupon."

"Come on. You can do it."

So I looked to be sure none of our friends were there to recognize my faux pas, slipped quickly through the door, and in a muffled voice, said, "Look, we were just passing by and decided on pizza. I . . . I don't have a . . ."

"You don't have a coupon, do you?"

"I could go get one." She was young enough for me to be her father. This was embarrassing. Me, in my mid-50s and trying to buy pizza without a coupon. I must have looked as though I just came from another planet.

"Sir," now I felt really old, "I have a coupon just for you." She discreetly slipped a coupon from under the counter. I felt like I was 14 and trying to buy a girlie magazine from my mother.

There, there, old-timer, there's no need to pay full price for a pizza. This is a new century. We're not food, we're a commodity now.

Compare pizza with Wilson Air Center, the folks who serve general aviation at the Memphis airport and were recently voted the number one fixed-base operator in the world. Do we ask what the price of fuel is at Wilson Air Center? Do we care? No, because fuel is only part of the product. At Wilson Air Center the product is all wrapped up in service, and price becomes a nonissue. And if we're refueling in that part of the world, it's a given—we're stopping at Wilson!

Once when we stopped, they were serving Frito pie in the pilots' lounge. Another time our plane was marshaled right up to a huge grill, where the smell of old-fashioned hot dogs was mixed with the heady vapors of Jet A fuel (a heavenly combo if you are inclined to fly!).

You might say we are loyal Wilson Air customers. Wilson Air has created an "I can't get this anywhere else but here" feeling, and we love to stop for whatever surprise they might have on the grill.

What is it that customers are loyal to? The loyalty factors! Lots of things shape customer loyalty. Here's the list of loyalty factors we were able to dream up:

- Price: low or high
- Convenience: make it easy to buy
- Product excellence
- Product leadership
- Operational excellence
- Relationship
- Cost of defection
- Other customers
- Trusted partnership
- Value through knowledge

Price

Buns said, "It's a Brighton," to which I said, "It's a belt."

Anybody that tells you customers aren't price sensitive doesn't live in the real world. But customers can be as sensitive to low prices as they are to high ones. Do you really think someone would want a Brighton belt for under $5? I think not. The value of the Brighton belt lies in its being pricier than most.

Convenience

Convenience creates resistance to change. If you make buying from you easy, I will be resistant to change. Southwest Airlines pioneered online reservations and ticketing; and the other airlines soon followed. Now you can even get your boarding pass online. The downside for SWA is that online service was easy to copy, and even though other airlines were only me-too imitators, being first doesn't matter to the flying public.

> **Thinking Point**
> *The best service differences are those that are difficult to duplicate.*

Product Excellence

If you have what is clearly the best product, you may have a loyalty advantage. I say *may have* because having an excellent product may not be important to the customer. Take, for example, gasoline. To the driving public, is one refiner's additive better than another's? Do you notice a difference when you top off with a brand that is not your usual one?

> **Thinking Point**
> *If you have the best product and the customer doesn't know it, you have no advantage.*

Adding features to a product that remain unknown or not understood by the customer only adds to the cost, not to the value.

Product Leadership

Having exclusive products or features doesn't guarantee a competitive advantage. If the customer doesn't care about your point of difference, the customer will neither be anchored by it nor be willing to pay for it. Having the latest and greatest seems to matter most with these two products: athletic shoes and popular music.

Operational Excellence

This dimension isn't as likely to build loyalty as it is to cost loyalty. Although customers often come for price, they leave because of feelings. And it is the little operational "oopses" that add up to lost customers. I already referred to these as microinsults, little lapses of service so small that they barely come up on the radar screen but, when added together, create an overall impression that your place is not a good place for business.

We were trying a new physician, a world-renowned neurologist whose skills as a diagnostician and surgeon unfortunately far exceeded his office management skills. Dial the office and you get a long 58 seconds of voice messaging, ending ironically with "for immediate assistance please press zero." Yep, that's what I'd call *immediate!* And you think I'm going to let this guy whittle on my brain? Not even!

(I read that 82 percent of customers say they make part of their buying decision based on how the phone is answered, yet 70 percent of companies have automated answering systems! Nearly three decades ago I called the office, heard a voice from Heaven, and married her! Don't tell me the voice on the phone doesn't matter!)

> **T** h i n k i n g **P** o i n t
>
> *What operational microinsults could you eliminate?*

Relationship

Relationship is a good term, but the words *customer intimacy* might be better. How much could you know about your customer that would, if put to use, improve loyalty?

We stayed at a beautiful new Hampton Inn in Westlake, California. It wasn't the Ritz, but we were treated as though it were the Ritz. When we entered our room, my eyes were drawn to the nightstand, where waited a complimentary bottle of water and a package of Doritos. I was thrilled; I'm a man of simple tastes!

How did the Hampton do that? Simple! I am a member of the Hilton Honors program, and this property was notified via computer that I prefer water and Doritos. (The Ritz would no doubt bring me Cheez-Its, my all-time favorite.) Speaking of the Ritz, I have a hundred dollars that says if someone at the Ritz reads this, my Cheez-It fetish will be noted in its computer, and at the next visit I make to the Ritz, whether it be Naples, Italy, or Naples, Florida, I'll have Cheez-Its there for the taking!

Signature Flight Support knows I use 15-50 motor oil in my airplane; the people there know my tail number, and they know both pilot (me) and "nagigator" (Buns's self-declared title) by name. Million Air in Cincinnati knows we always have the fuel topped off, and Showalter Flying Service in Orlando knows we're coming even before we call for a rental car.

This is the age of the computer. You may as well use it!

> ### T h i n k i n g P o i n t
>
> *What could you know about your customers, and*
> *how could you make that information available?*

Cost of Defection

Sometimes a customer can get so wrapped up that it costs too much to leave. Think of all those cassette tapes you have in the closet. They were fine in their day, but did the Beach Boys really sound so . . . you know, cool?

Cost of defection can mean much more than the hard costs. There is the cost of learning a new system or getting acquainted with a new order department. Use all the costs of leaving as leverage to hold on to your existing customers.

> ### T h i n k i n g P o i n t
>
> *What cost-of-defection advantage do you have over your*
> *competition, and how might you exploit it?*

Other Customers

I'll laugh behind your back if I see you paying big bucks for the privilege of advertising Tommy Hilfiger on your pants. Yet when Stuart handed me a crisp, new John Deere hat, I immediately set it aside for special occasions. "I see you drive a Deere. Yep, I got one, too!"

The truth is that much of what passes as customer loyalty really is *customer* loyalty. Customers become loyal to one another, like a club.

> ### T h i n k i n g P o i n t
>
> *How could you encourage customers to talk*
> *and show loyalty to the group?*

Trusted Partnership

Can I trust you to put my need to solve a problem over your need to make a sale? This is the classic, "You don't need a new one, you just need to replace the belt." If there is a single best way to create customer loyalty, it is to unsell something.

When customers ask for more than they need and you tell them the truth, they'll know you value their long-term business over a short-term sale.

> **T** *h i n k i n g* **P** *o i n t*
>
> *How could you engineer unselling into the process?*

Value through Knowledge

If you are a geek, then no doubt you've attended a user conference. If you're not a geek, then a user conference is not a sign of addiction. Since dirt, software providers have offered conferences to help their users—that is, their customers—understand the finer points of their products.

You needn't be a purveyor of software to offer user education. Saturn has done it with automobiles by offering weekend courses on how to change the oil, swap out a wiper blade, and cure an ailing brake light.

Knowledge is a unique form of added value.

> **T** *h i n k i n g* **P** *o i n t*
>
> *How could you add value through knowledge?*

EMS

I was surprised when the speaker said, "Above all, the victim of an accident wants a medic who cares." He went on to say that the next most important thing is a good appearance. But what about training and skills? What about the ability to insert an airway adjunct or the availability of an AED? Nope, lying there at the side of the road, bleeding like a stuck pig, a victim wants a medic who cares and looks good.

And there lies the story of great customer service: It doesn't matter what you think customers want unless what you think *is* what they want. Service, after all, is defined by the served. We were equally surprised when we asked the folks in the auto repair business what it is that floats their customers' boat. Was it certified technicians? No. Using only original equipment parts? Uh-uh. Give up? It was having the vehicle ready when promised.

The point is simple: Unless you ask the customer what is important, you may spend tons of time and a pile of dollars, and still fall short of the mark. Yes, we *are* missing the mark. According to a survey by the University of Michigan Business School, customer satisfaction dropped 7.9 percent in the six short years between 1994 and 2000. I don't think that number, by itself, is enough to tell the story. Are we really doing a poorer job or has the bar been somehow raised? I think it's the latter.

In a highly mobile society, customers are more likely to have a wider range of experience. Last week at dinner we were surprised to hear a young boy at a nearby table—he looked about eight—tell the server, "I'd like a half order of fries; and when you refill my soda, no ice, please."

No ice, please? When I was a kid, I would have been so thrilled just to be eating out that I would never have ventured to say "No ice, please." Today's customer has far higher expectations. Still, if that's the game, you had better learn to play. And that means you had better learn to ask, to talk to your customers, and to know them better than the competition.

Retention Hall

If you could know which of your customers were the next to leave, what would you do? Would you call them and ask what the matter is? And if there were a problem, how much would you be willing to spend to keep them from jumping ship? I'll answer that. You'd spend at least as much as you would have to spend to replace them. In fact, companies that measure and reward customer retention are 60 percent more profitable!

And here's another fact. If unhappy customers aren't talking to you, they are talking to someone else! According to research done by SOCAP (Society of Consumer Affairs Professionals), 58 percent of folks who called a company's consumer affairs hotline with a problem usually told three or more others about the problem. To fix a problem, you have to know about it, and to know about it you have to do more than just listen—you have to ask.

By the way, your most vocal customers are often among the most loyal. Customers who take the time and spend the energy to complain are in effect saying, "I really want to remain your customer if only you will fix my problem." Unfortunately, fewer customers are brand loyal. Maybe that's because it's easier to switch than fight. Carlson Marketing Group surveyed consumers in 2000 and discovered that four of ten customers could be considered brand committed. A short one year later, that already pitiful number had sunk to a mere three in ten!

Ask Not . . .

Customer feedback in the age of the World Wide Web is easy and it's cheap. Check out <www.Planetfeedback.com>, <www.InsightEx press.com>, <www.recipio.com>, and <www.websurveyor.com>. Whatever you do, don't ask customers unless you really want to know and are prepared to respond intelligently.

Fifteen weeks ago I wrote a polite letter of complaint to a well-known store that sells cookware and waited months to receive a response. Which do you suppose would be worse: never hear at all or receive a letter of apology in tomorrow's mail that would be roughly a dozen weeks too late?

If you are going to create avenues for listening, you had better create an avenue for responding!

POLITICAL CLIMATE

Even though attitudes of employees and customers are largely influenced by the values and experiences of their youth, they are also tempered by the values and experiences of the times. It may be true that the workforce has absorbed the lesson that few companies have little or no loyalty to the troops. As a result, the troops seem to be willing to stay only until the next paycheck.

Seth Godin, the author who has caught the ear of Gens X and Y in *Fast Company,* practically shouts, "Quit your job . . . Do it slow, or do it fast, but do it." In an economy in which 69,000 jobs are disappearing every month, Godin may have a point. Technology has brought about the shrinking of the middle class. Job security is out the window, and it's not a surprise that the job market is every man and every hyphen-ated-woman for themselves.

Loyalty to the boss may still be possible but loyalty to the company? Fageddaboudit. Right, wrong, or indifferent, this is the emotional tone of the workforce as well as of the market and old ideals. Old ideals such as loyalty are completely out the window.

To wrap up our discussion (for now) on corporate loyalty, check out this actual experience: As a customer of 13 years with well over a million dollars dispersed, a credit card customer had a small problem. In the interest of airline miles, this small business owner made a major purchase on her credit card. When an opportunity to invest in a new venture claimed more than she had expected, she decided to let her credit card balance ride for a month, which was not her custom, and paid less than the full balance owed. Unfortunately, the interest rate was double-digit in a single-digit economy, so it made sense to her to ask for a lower rate, at least for a short time.

"Yes, ma'am, I can lower that rate to 12.1 percent for three months." "That's way too steep."

"Sorry. That's as low as we can go." "May I speak to a supervisor?"

After explaining the request to the supervisor, she was told she could go to 6.9 percent. "That's as low as we can go." "But you're advertising 3.9 percent for new customers." But "that's for balances transferred. We can't offer you that rate. If you'd like to open up a new account, I can offer you that rate, but we can't transfer the balance from this account to it."

"Doesn't our account record note that we're a very long-term customer and that we have paid our balance in full with rare exception? Doesn't that count for something? All I'm requesting is a grace period for three months." "Sorry. We're unable to help you." "Fine. For now I'll take the 6.9 percent because I've worked so hard to get it. But understand this. Despite our 13-year history, I'm going to shop. There's another company out there who would love to have a dependable, no-risk customer like me."

What were they thinking?

16

CUSTOMER RETENTION

A speaker's bureau called to complain that I had altered its contract.

"But that's the industry standard," whined the agent, obviously upset. Naturally, I answered, "So?"

Whatever the standards are in your industry, your only rational response should be, "So?" We worked with a manufacturer of outdoor power equipment and were appalled to notice that every day its dealers would spend an eternity wheeling out equipment awaiting repair to create walking room in the showroom. Before closing, the parade would reverse and the showroom would be restocked with dirt and grass-covered lawn equipment.

"Why don't you repair the same number of machines you take in every day? If no machine stayed in the shop more than 24 or even 48 hours, you could turn the labor that you've burned to move equipment into labor sold for repairing equipment."

"I don't know. That's just standard for the industry."

We worked with an international restaurant chain whose top executives were in a quandary over the shortage of qualified unit managers.

"How many hours does the average manager work?" I asked, even though I knew the answer from experience.

"A minimum of 55 but the average is close to 60."

Hmmm, I wonder why folks aren't jumping at this job! Long hours are, after all, standard for the industry.

Who is setting standards for your industry?

We have the hotel chains to thank for the rapid rise in popularity of cell phones. They have ripped off business travelers to the tune of a buck a call, a standard for the industry, making cell phones look like a bargain.

It's fun to watch auto dealers attempt to promote their all-new express service that promises to change your oil in a matter of minutes. It used to be the lesser of two evils; you could either drop off your car or resign yourself to a long wait with old magazines. Why complain? It's the standard. But the ten-minute oil and lube guys came along and changed the standards. And now the dealerships are hustling to make up ground they never should have lost.

Kia, the scrappy car company from Korea with the uncertain quality standards, turned around when it changed the standards. Out went the three-year standard warranty and in came a new standard—ten years! And the race is on.

If you insist on sticking to the standards, you had better make certain that no one is sticking to higher standards . . . and that includes those outside your industry.

> **T**hinking **P**oint
>
> *Change the standards before someone changes them for you.*

CUSTOMERS VOTE WITH THEIR FEET

Customers vote every day with their feet. The polling booth is a little thing called a cash register, and every time you spend a buck, that buck gets counted as yet another positive affirmation. Like Sally Fields at the Oscars, all those wrinkledy dollars are shouting, "You like me. You really do like me!"

If you want to make customer service better, stop doing business with folks who aren't treating *you* like a customer! You might complain about Wal-Mart, but you probably still manage to spend a lot of money at the house that Sam built. You harp over the demise of customer service, yet you can't remember the last time you paid extra for someone to top off your tank. (Young readers are thinking, "You could do that?")

Once you get out of the business of accepting poor service, you have to grow into the habit of actually seeking those who are willing to cater to you. *And* you have to make the conscious decision to pay for better-than-average service.

Here are a four good questions to consider:

1. How much further would you be willing to drive to get great service?
2. How much longer would you be willing to wait?
3. How much more would you be willing to pay?
4. Are you a good customer?
   - Have you ever attempted to exchange an item at a store where you did not make the purchase?
   - Have you ever attempted to get service on an item that was out of warranty?
   - Have you ever lied about age in order to get a discount?
   - If you really need something by Friday, do you tell the server your deadline is Wednesday?
   - Have you ever slipped extra sugar packets into your purse?

If you are feeling guilty, 91 percent of Americans say they lie regularly, and a whopping 25 percent say that for $10 million they would abandon their family. Compared to that, what are a few sugar packets?

CUT THE CATALOGS

Buns dragged in the mail from Saturday's delivery to our post office box and set half of it in the recycle bin. Heavy, four-color catalogs arrive at our house by the dozen. Cabela's announced it was spring; Craftsman reminded me that Father's Day was approaching; Galls showed up in time to make Christmas bright for your favorite firefighter/paramedic; and Levenger was dropped on my desk in case there might be an idea for my birthday.

Farmers who used to plant or harvest by the phase of the moon could easily substitute the ebb and flow of catalogs to mark the seasons. Yet the retailers are losing their backsides! Why? Because they overestimate the value of a customer.

In the time it has taken to write the last few paragraphs, a new load of catalogs has arrived, Monday's delivery! On top of my pile is an aviation catalog from which I had purchased a $1,500 backup GPS unit six years ago but nothing since. I love the products, and the service is swell, but I own everything I need or expect to need for our little airplane. How will the company know when to remove me from the list?

Next in the pile is a minicatalog from a Seattle photo-processing lab that offers great quality and convenient service. I used to be what must be considered a heavy user. Since Buns bought me a digital camera, the old SLR 35mm hasn't left the shelf. When will the company realize I am no longer a hot prospect?

> **T** *h i n k i n g* **P** *o i n t*
>
> *Previous profitability is no guarantee of future*
> *profitability nor is it a reliable predictor.*

Chasing a nonloyal customer who was initially profitable, perhaps very profitable, is a fool's errand. In fact, chasing too hard can cost you a customer.

We just received a Victoria's Secret catalog—again! Even I'm getting that "ho-hum, just another seminaked model in the mailbox" feeling. Chasing too hard can cause numbness to set in, and your marketing loses the impact we like to associate with multiple impressions.

It's obvious that treating all customers alike is going to cost you profits so here's what to do for these category shoppers:

- Price shoppers. They need your product but only at a price. Make a healthy profit on every sale or wave good-bye.
- Regular shoppers. They like you and your products, so keep in touch and keep them as profitable customers. Deep discounting is a waste, and you risk training them to buy only "on deal."
- Occasional shoppers. This is not a great customer-product fit. Don't call them; they'll call you. And offer them no special deals.
- Dealers. They need you and you need them. Work on upselling and don't overdiscount for volume.

Your employees won't be able to help you differentiate between the above groups of customers until they at least have a rudimentary idea of the financial model of the business. For the real test, ask them how much owners take to the bank. When you can breathe again, read on!

100 Pennies

Imagine that you work for minimum wage. The first thing in the morning you watch the boss unlock the safe, count and bundle a large stack of bills, and head for the bank. Right after the midday rush, the boss repeats the process, only this time the stack of bills is even larger.

Business is good, right? The boss is rolling in bucks, right? Maybe. While the employees are whispering about the large piles of cash, what they fail to see is that stack of envelopes with the little see-through windows sent compliments of the insurance company, the utility guys, the tax districts, and a host of friendly folks who want their share of the pile the boss just took to the bank.

One afternoon after my usual bank run, I watched an employee deposit a handful of ketchup packets into a bag of carry-out food.

"Hey! You're giving away all the profit!"

"Aw, what are a few packets of ketchup anyway?"

"How much do you think we make on an order of fries?"

He named the price. "No, that's the price. How much are the profits?" I looked at two eyes that had started to glaze over. "When we sell an order of fries how much do we get to keep?"

"All of it," insisted the kid whose head was not warm all the way around. "I just watched you take it to the bank."

When business slowed, I assembled most of the crew and counted 100 pennies onto the counter. "Let's say a customer spends $1 with us. How many pennies would that be?" Even the slow ones got this.

"Now, when that big truck brings us our food delivery, about how much do we pay for food that we sell for a dollar?" The crew was dumbfounded that we would have to pay, but some of them took a stab at the answer.

"Ten cents?"

"A dime?" Some folks are quicker than others.

I scooped about a third of the pennies from the counter saying, "Nope, the biggest part of that dollar goes to our suppliers. Can anybody think of who else gets a piece?"

Together we whipped off a list that included rent, uniforms, advertising, and, finally, someone mentioned payroll. "What! You mean I have to pay you guys?" amid loud, nervous laughter.

"Look what I have left. Why, it must be a nickel! I'm rich! I'm rich! I'm rich! Uh-oh, this genius here decides to flirt with a cutie in the drive-through and give her a little extra ketchup. Does anybody know how much a ketchup packet costs?"

"A nickel?"

"Close enough!" I whip the remaining five cents from the counter and waited for the slow group to catch up.

"Boss?"

"Yes?"

"I gave her four packets. Where do the other nickels come from?"

"Ta da! You are brilliant! They come from here!" I turned a pocket inside out. "Uh-oh! I have no money. I must have lost it on an order of chicken tenders when someone counted out one too many. I know! I can take it from payroll!"

"Boss?"

"Yes?"

"Sorry."

It is not the fault of employees when they fail to understand the financial structure of your business. Profit and loss is not something they are going to learn at home unless their parents are union organizers. Sometimes the boss must be willing to double as parent.

And what other facts of life must you teach? How about the cost of acquiring a new customer? How about the lifetime value of a customer you already have? How about teaching employees the value of energy conservation, the payoff for working safely, and the responsibility for being honest, always?

And how about cutting them a little slack because there are some things that are simply your responsibility to teach?

> **T** *h i n k i n g* **P** *o i n t*
>
> *What could you do to help your employees*
> *understand profit and loss?*

An Optometrist Fired Me!

A few months ago a friend of ours ordered a new fancy pair of glasses, the progressive lens with nonglare glass. She needed them in time for a speaking engagement and wanted to make great eye contact without the glare hitting her lenses. The store personnel assured her that they would be in on time.

Living in the country, it is not her practice to drive into town without a specific purpose, but because she was assured that the glasses would be there, off she went to pick up her new, fancy glasses.

When my friend arrived, she was informed that the glasses weren't there and were going to take an extra week because of the nonreflective coating. A bit perturbed, but far from angry, she made her disappointment clear as no one had told her it would take extra time. Worse was the fact that no one had taken the time to call to inform her that the glasses would not be delivered when expected. She also asked if they could guarantee that they would be ready by the following promised date and was assured there would be no problem.

A week later my friend returned as scheduled. That's right, no glasses, no call, and, worse yet, no apology. She told the young lady to cancel her order and refund her credit card. "Fine," was the complete response from the clerk.

My friend immediately went to see the competition, told her story, and in less than a week received her glasses at a lower price! She also received a phone call from the manager of the first optometrist's shop, a very professional young woman who introduced herself and apologized for the trouble with the order.

"After explaining that it wasn't just the order that had offended me, I relayed what truly offended me: She, as the manager, had obviously been trained what to say and do with a disgruntled customer, but that same training was never given to the hourly employee, training needed to save customers before they became angered. She asked for my business back, which I politely, but firmly, declined."

"Now I have a wonderful relationship with my new eyeglass company and would never consider recommending or returning to Brand X. I also tell this story every chance I get! The power of one—it's infinite."

Bust My Business!

Sandy Phillips passed along this story: "Last October I returned from my Saturday morning errands to a voice mail from the local video store stating that I needed to call them regarding my account. Because I seldom rent videos now that my children are teenagers, I figured one of them might have tried to rent something without my permission.

"I immediately returned the call and asked for the young lady who had left her name and claimed to be the manager. After being transferred to her, she informed me that I had rented a movie in June, and it had been returned late. Confused, I asked what movie I had rented. When she gave me the title, I remembered renting it but asked if she was sure it had been turned in late. She answered it had been turned in *one* day late.

"Shocked, I responded by asking, 'Let me understand this correctly. I rented a movie in June that you say was turned in one day late, and you are calling me in October for me to pay for it? How much are we talking about anyway?' I believe her answer was $2.09 cents followed by a threat that if I didn't pay 'I would be unable to rent any more videos from them.'

"Again, shocked, I asked, 'Are you saying that for $2.09 cents, you are willing to lose my business of 15 years on a permanent basis?' Her response was simple, 'Yes.'

"Obviously, she has succeeded, but not until I called corporate, found her regional manager, found out that she was not the manager as she had claimed and was offered several free video rentals and no charge for any late fees that may or may not have been incurred.

"I never used the free video rental offer and have never returned to the store. When one gets 'fired,' it's best to clean out the desk and never look back."

CUSTOMER TRAINING OR STUPID CUSTOMER TRICKS

I had my eyes opened this weekend big time. I knew service was bad, but gee whiz! Hang with me as we review my service experiences, and I promise you will change the way you do business.

My first stop was the auto show. Every known brand had vehicles bumper to bumper at the convention center. Because there were too many to see, Buns and I worked our short list. It was almost time to buy another vehicle so we targeted the Toyota 4Runner, the fabled Ford Explorer, and the new kid on the block, the Honda Pilot.

At Toyota we were free to open doors, test out seats and accessories, and generally get to know the vehicle. When we had questions, a product specialist in the form of an attractive young woman chatted knowledgeably about the vehicle. If you had questions about available colors, she had the answer. If you wanted to delve deeper and discuss the horsepower and torque differences between the six and the eight, no problem. She had the answers.

At Ford the popular four-door model was locked and left to spin monotonously on a carousel. No touching, please! So we tried the two-door, a model entirely ill suited for us. A salesman in western wear pushed a card at us, saying, "I'd be happy to sell you one of these!" His product knowledge was no deeper than the paint on the hood.

Honda had the best-looking vehicle. The Pilot is loaded with features but the show staff? They were nowhere to be found. I guess if you've got a hot vehicle, maybe it sells itself.

So our weekend started with questions.

We stopped at Hastings, our local bookstore, for the latest copy of *American Demographics.* I looked and Buns double-checked; no *American*

Demographics. Kerrville is a small town so you can hardly expect them to carry the title. But we were there, so why not ask?

"Excuse me! Can you tell me if you carry *American Demographics?*"

"What kind of magazine is it?"

"It's a business magazine."

"Did you look in the business section?" Duh!

What on God's green earth was he thinking?

Saturday we tried Barnes & Noble in the big city of San Antonio and found our magazine on the first try. With time to burn we decided to browse. Women browse by topic, men browse by title. Okay, I don't really know that to be true, but it is true that people have different shopping styles. Given five minutes at a Borders or a Barnes & Noble, Buns will head straight for the thriller novels to browse. Me? I conjure up my current list of wanted titles and go on a targeted search.

Hmmm, if I could only get my hands on the Barnes & Noble computer, I wouldn't have to wait for the girl with the tongue stud to get off the phone to look up my list. So after a three-minute wait, I'm out the door heading straight for Amazon.com.

At Best Buy we had two items on the list, an upright freezer and a large-screen TV. Winter is approaching and we're moving the act indoors. So we'll need lots of food and mindless entertainment. In the appliance department Sal jumped off the forklift to see if we needed help selecting the freezer.

"Where are you going to put this?" It was an odd question, but Sal plowed on saying, "If you are going to put this in the house, either of the two you are looking at will do fine. But if you are going to put it in the garage where it gets hot in the summer, you're going to need one with a fan to cool the compressor." All the while Sal was wrestling a 15-cubic-foot model away from the wall so he could point at the compressor to show us why.

Good questions, Sal! You didn't wait for me to ask because you anticipated that I hadn't a clue—and you were right! "We'll take it!" At this point anything Sal recommends is now automatically approved by us!

In the TV department I noticed three middle-aged men, which included me, who were shopping with a tape measure! Who'd guess that you select a television based on where it will fit? It turns out that consumers want to squeeze the largest screen into the smallest space. Those of us who bought furniture before big TVs are now trying to get the 36-inch model into the same cabinet where we have our current, formerly humongous 25-inch set! Ain't no way, Jose! It's too wide!

Hint: If you were a manufacturer of television sets, should you put the speakers on the side of the set or on the bottom? If they were on the bottom, the screen could be larger and the sound would not be compressed against the cabinet! If you sold televisions, what information would you put on the display tags? Why, set dimensions, of course! Best Buy does this, although the type is way too small for middle-aged guys to see. So we measured and measured in search of a theater-sized screen that will sit on a dime.

Around the corner is a Toys R Us where on the day we visited many things were being done right: face painting near the checkout and in the boys section you could build a wooden train engine. Across the aisle you could see firsthand how Barbie had evolved over the years. Lots of things were done just right.

Now tell me. At a store with a name like Toys R Us, what would you expect the response to be if you asked, "I have a five-year-old granddaughter who likes music and games. Can you tell me what would make her say wow this Christmas?" Or "Do you have a list of the top-selling toys for five-year-old girls in various price ranges?" You'd think they would rattle off the information, or perhaps just smile and hand you a printed list of suggestions. You'd think, but you'd be wrong.

And it's not just the big chains. A few blocks down the street I asked,

"What do you have for my son who is in his mid-30s and seems to own everything? Any recommendations?"

"Look around." (Be still, my heart!)

I saw a locked display case that contained miniature radio-controlled cars.

"What's this?" I asked, as I rattled the glass in case I was wrong about the display being locked.

"Those are the next big thing in radio-controlled models," droned Mr. Personality.

"Cool! Do you have a demo model? I'd like to see one in action."

"No."

"I bet if you had a demo model, you'd sell these by the dozen."

"Maybe." Then he added just so he could be right, "They seem to be selling pretty good without the demo." I bought one anyway. When I got to the car and thought what my son would do with one hot radio-controlled car, I returned to the store and bought a second. Mr. Happy took my second 45 bucks. As I turned to leave, he looked over the top of his glasses and managed to say, "See?"

Here are a few questions for you: What questions do your customers have that perhaps aren't being answered? Why would you take the time to hire (forget train!) employees who are going to send customers to your competition with unanswered questions? What could you do to anticipate customer questions? How could you get customers so involved with the product that it would sell itself?

> **T** *h i n k i n g* **P** *o i n t*
>
> *How could you make your sales process more*
> *proactive without being high pressured?*

CUSTOMER TRAINING PROGRAMS?

"Six or 12?" I looked to see who owned the voice that was calling to me but saw only an old man parked on a stool behind a nearby counter. He seemed to be mesmerized by a basketball game unfolding one second at a time on a small TV hung on the back wall. Then I heard it again, "Six or 12?" and saw his lips move though his head didn't.

I was at Dreamland Barbeque in beautiful Tuscaloosa. As a first-timer, I had no idea that my choice was a simple 6 or 12 ribs served with an ample serving of white bread to sop up the sauce. I wanted ribs but I needed training!

Years ago when our budget was very tight, we learned that the local family steakhouse offered a coupon every other week for a Thursday night special. So if it was Wednesday and we were hungry for steak, we'd wait because we knew that either tomorrow or a week from tomorrow there would be a coupon. We were trained!

Air travelers have learned, by training, to use the boarding pass kiosks rather than wait in line at the counter. It's faster and more convenient.

As a pilot, I've learned to take off under visual flight rules and pick up my clearance once airborne rather than waiting in a line of IFR departures on the ground. It's called gaming the system, in pilot-speak.

> **T** *h i n k i n g* **P** *o i n t*
>
> *How much time and effort could you save with a*
> *simple customer training program? And how have your*
> *customers already learned to game the system?*

17

SERVICE RECOVERY

A customer became very upset at a big-box pharmacy after returning to the counter only to discover that her prescription was not ready as promised. (The pharmacy was waiting on a phone call from the prescribing doctor to authorize the refill.) While the pharmacist was filling a prescription, he overheard the complaining customer and called to the clerk, "Are you doing anything special for her as a way of making amends?"

"No," was the one-word response from the clerk. "Well, go out there and wow her. Tell her that the prescription will be free today." The response from the clerk this time was totally nonverbal, eliciting nothing more than an are-you-kidding-me look. The clerk returned to the counter and said without emotion, "The pharmacist says that your prescription is going to be free today."

From the pharmacist's vantage point, the pharmacy would score huge points with this now smiling and very happy customer. Unfortunately, the smile didn't last long. The customer's expression instantly turned to anger as the shocked pharmacist heard the clerk add, "It's free . . . but it's really not our fault!"

The pharmacist who shared this story shook his head in bewilderment, saying, "The clerk took him to Heaven and then brought him right back!" I know he was thinking . . . "What was she thinking?"

CHEAP COSTS

We discovered an amazing thing. Most employees believe that it is their job to protect the company from the customer. In customer-centered companies, things work the other way around, and employees see their role as protecting customers from those little irritations that cause pain. Visit the courtesy desk of any big-box discounter, and chances are you'll be puzzled why the discounter elected to name it the "courtesy desk." Courtesy is often in extremely short supply. In many stores the courtesy desk would be more aptly named the "suspicion desk." "Why are you here? What are you trying to scam us for? Did you really buy that here? Are you sure it was broken when you opened the package or did you drop it . . . maybe even on purpose?"

Sure, there are customers who are rip-off artists, but that's why God created hell! They'll get theirs in the process of trying to get yours. But why offend a hundred honest, well-intentioned customers in an attempt to protect yourself from the slime ball who's going to get to you anyway?

Losing a good customer to bad policy is not cost-effective. It's dumb. You need a better plan and here it is. I recommend that you go on a scavenger hunt of your operation and try to spot all the little things that really irritate customers. Little things, such as an employee-of-the-month parking space that sits empty while customers walk from the far stretches of the lot. Or maybe it's as simple as being left on hold too long. And doesn't it just gripe you to be told that something that should be really common is out of stock?

When things have gotten out of hand, remember these four simple points:

1. Get angry—with the customer.
2. Ask the customer for a solution.
3. Take the customer to your leader.
4. Never pass the buck.

Get angry *with,* but never *at,* the customer. If you become angry about the same thing that makes the customer angry, it's almost impossible for the customer to be angry with you! You should get even angrier than the customer. This is so powerful that on many occasions I've had customers attempt to calm me down! Ask the customer what it will take to make things right. We've discovered that in most cases the customer will ask you for less than you would have settled for. Get it? The easiest, and usually the cheapest, solution comes from simply saying that you are sorry and asking the customer what it will take to set things right.

"I'm so sorry this happened. But now that things have gone wrong, what can we do right now to make things better?" Most of the time, customers are so happy to hear you quickly and freely admit that you goofed that they don't ask for anything!

> **T** *h i n k i n g* **P** *o i n t*
>
> *Customers will ask for less than you would have settled for after you negotiate with them. And customers who have never had a complaint are not as loyal as customers who have had a complaint that was successfully resolved!*

Only the manager should have the authority to say no to a customer. Everyone else should be responsible for finding ways to say yes. If a customer is asking for something you just can't approve, don't hassle; just take him or her to the boss. "I'm really not authorized to approve this. Would you mind if we talked to my boss?" Take the customer to the boss before the customer thinks of asking.

Whatever you do, *never pass the buck.* When a customer comes to you with a problem, you own it. Never say, "That's not my job." Never suggest that a customer ask someone else. And if you truly are unable to solve the problem, the problem still belongs to you until someone else takes ownership.

Angry customers aren't bad people. They just have a problem that, with a little understanding and sometimes a bit of creativity, you can solve . . . and turn difficult customers into friends! Some customers as we've noted, will try to rip you off, but most only want to be treated fairly. When you discover you're being scammed, you're no longer dealing with a customer. Scammers are thieves. Invite them to go elsewhere.

While working with a major player in the home-center business, I was shocked to observe what must be a typical transaction:

"I'd like to return this faucet. It doesn't fit my new sink. I bought them both here, but the receipt was missing from the bag."

"I'm sorry, you'll have to find the receipt before we can give you credit."

"But I bought everything for the entire remodeling job right here in this store. I spent several thousand, and everything has been fine except now the faucet won't fit!"

We asked permission of the clerk to try and resolve the problem. It turned out that the problem wasn't with the faucet; it was missing a set screw, a part that cost all of nothing. We walked the customer over to the hardware aisle, fished a replacement screw out of the bin, and sent him happily on his way.

What would it have cost to handle the customer according to policy? Apart from future lost sales that could have been considerable, had the customer gone home, rummaged through the trash, and found the receipt to qualify for an exchange, the store would have had to go through the expense of storing and returning the so-called damaged merchandise and then tracking the paperwork to ensure it was properly credited! All this would be far costlier than simply saying, "We're sorry. What can we do to make this right?"

"Well, if you happen to have an extra set screw . . ."

Cheap costs!

Almost Good Service

I was in the North Star Mall in San Antonio at opening. A few feet inside the door I encountered a pleasant salesperson, told her exactly what I wanted, and within seconds found myself holding the perfect gifts for my wife. So far, this was a wow! The salesperson made a few suggestions that felt more like good service than a hard sell, so I added to the order; still a wow! Then I was offered free gift wrapping and, being a typical male, didn't have to think hard before saying yes. Wow! I entertained myself browsing through an electronics store, returned to the original store, and found my packages were waiting. Perfect!

Recognizing a possible opportunity for a mistake, I verified the contents of the wrapped packages and started the hour-long drive home. Shopping done; great parking space; excellent service; I beat the crowd.

Almost. My cell phone rang, and I was informed that I had an electric mixer in one of my packages, a nice item but not what I purchased. Now, here's what I expected: I would return to the mall and not find a parking space. I was right about that and left Buns to circle endlessly while I returned to the store to make the switch. It took 30 minutes to get back to the store, where I expected to walk in, make the exchange, maybe receive an apology, and be out the door.

Wrong. My exchange package was not waiting as I expected. I waited, maybe 10 minutes, and finally someone appeared with my package and an apology. I said, "Anybody can make a mistake. I don't mind the mistake. I don't even mind the hassle of returning to the mall. It's Christmas and you can expect that traffic is going to be bad. But I really expected to walk in, pick up the correct package, and walk right out. I should not have had to wait for you to wrap another package as you knew I was coming right back to the store."

Good merchandising, great hiring, on-target suggestion selling, but the store's gotta work on service recovery. So I wrote a letter addressed to the CEO and politely expressed my disappointment. Then I waited and I waited and I waited. Several months passed without a response.

Just for grins I decided to follow up even though the CEO didn't. I sent this:

Monday, June 30, 2003
DH (CEO)
Just Curious . . .

. . . I wrote you a polite letter of complaint on the 5th of December and never heard from you.

What do you do with complaint letters? Are they shipped off to a special department or tossed, or do you handle them personally?

Best to you!

And got this via e-mail:

Dear Mr. Gross:

I received your letter today and have to apologize. Mr. H. left the Company on 1/9/03 and I do not know how your letter was handled at that time. I also believe that it was Mr. H.'s practice to not follow up with customers personally, but let our customer service staff handle the situation.

Regardless, I will try and track down who is handling your complaint, but in order to do so I unfortunately have to ask a few questions:

What concept did you order from? Was your order a store or catalog issue? And do you have your order number—not critical, but extremely helpful?

I am relatively new to this process, but will do my utmost to follow up.

Thank you, Bren

Cool! The response was immediate, foretold of action, and even asked for patience by citing, "I am relatively new to this process." I felt the company had redeemed itself so I responded with:

Thanks for the response . . . guess it was time for Mr. H. to
go. I appreciate your effort . . . let's call us even for now!
                                   Best to you!

Now most customer service folks would be thinking, "Yea! I dodged
another bullet, one less complainer to worry about." But not this gal.
She replied:

But wait—I can't let you do that. Please let me know what
happened—it's my theory that we can't learn/improve unless we
get feedback from our customers (other than the one lesson we
have already learned from the mistake of nonresponse).
                                   Bren

And I responded:

Hey, I'm impressed! Here is my original letter . . . not to
worry. My best friend on the planet loves everything you sell so
we are likely to be customers for life no matter what.
                                   Best to you!

Exceptional Service Recovery

Brandon Gale of the Eagle Postal Center in Dallas, Texas, was pre-
paring a presentation to the Associated Mail & Parcel Centers. In his
words, "This took a great deal of preparation and included handout
booklets for each of the more than 400 attendees. These booklets were
crucial in our making a successful presentation.

"We had used UPS 3-Day Select to ship the 140 pounds of booklets
to San Diego to arrive on Friday for our presentation early Saturday
morning. By 4 PM Friday our packages had not yet arrived and could
not be located *but* I did find Peter Benson with UPS.

"Within the hour Peter had located our shipment in Ontario, California, about an hour-and-a-half's drive from San Diego. It would not
be delivered until Monday.

"Peter said, "Don't worry, I'll figure out something." (This is the
good part.)

"Unbeknownst to us, Peter jumped into his car, drove all the way to
Ontario, got the packages, and returned to the hotel at 10 PM on Friday
night! Peter saved our day!"

FROM THE TOP

When things go wrong, nothing beats a sincere apology, and nothing beats hearing from the top dog so long as it is sincere.

Here's another example:

Dear Mr. Gross:

After learning all the details about the delay of flight 6 on January 15 from our manager in Maui, we can understand how frustrating this trip must have been. I am truly sorry for the length of time you waited . . . and waited . . . and waited.

As you know, the aircraft had a mechanical problem and returned to the gate for repairs. Simply, your safety is our primary concern. Although I am not a mechanic, I do know that sometimes aircraft repair work can become more complex with each step. At first, we were hopeful that the problem could be fixed quickly. I am sorry that turned out not to be the case.

In an effort to make amends to one of our best customers, I have credited your AAdvantage account with 15,000 Customer Service Bonus miles. You should see this adjustment on one of your next two summaries.

Our business relationship is important to us and we want to make certain that you will continue to travel with us often. Please be assured that we have recommitted ourselves to the issue of dependability. The next time you are comfortably seated aboard our aircraft, rest assured that we will do our very best to get you to your destination as planned.

William R. Hodges
American Airlines

Never mind that American Airlines tried to mend the fence with a credit of 15,000 miles to my AAdvantage account—I felt fully heard by the top brass. (And never mind that W. Hodges "in the Executive Office" probably works in the basement at DFW. I don't care!)

One of my readers shared a letter of apology she had received from the CEO of a vendor that had messed up royally. As you read, think about the results you might expect if you were the customer involved.

I spent the last several weeks personally reviewing each and every correspondence received from our customers over the past several months. We let our customers down when they relied on us most. While there is nothing I can say to mend what has already occurred, a sincere apology from me is certainly in order.

[A forthright explanation of problems with outside contractors followed]. Please accept our sincere apology for the disappointment of this past season and for our inability to appropriately respond in the aftermath. It will be my personal focus in the coming year to ensure nothing like this ever happens again.

Chief Executive Officer

Did the apology strike home? Read the reply from the customer:

I recently received your letter . . . regarding your sincerest apology for the failure to fulfill my order. I would like to say thank you for your apology; however, I have to disagree with your use of the word *sincere*.

The customer goes on to detail a horribly botched attempt to fill her order. After several compounding errors, the order, intended as a special gift, was never shipped.

So, now after receiving your letter, I find that it not only lacks sincerity by placing blame on a 3rd party vendor, it is also insulting to your customers . . . While there may be nothing you can say to mend what has already occurred, most customers feel actions speak louder than words. Your customers deserve more than just a form letter apology that you couldn't even personally sign. They deserve an incentive to use your company again. Word of mouth is the most powerful advertisement you have, and with this type of customer service there will surely be a lot of talking. Shame on you!

> **T** *h i n k i n g* **P** *o i n t*
>
> *Apologize from the top, make it sincere,*
> *and definitely outlaw form letters.*

So who is perfect and who would want to be? For perfect we can deal with machines and risk losing our own humanity in the process. Sometimes things just aren't going to go right. It should not be a problem so long as the fix is immediate and the apology comes both from the top . . . and from the heart.

> **T** h i n k i n g **P** o i n t
>
> *Have you made a plan for making things right*
> *when things go wrong, and does it have room for*
> *the system to be overruled by the heart?*

18

BUYPSY
How Smart Servers
Mess with Your Mind

There is a psychology of selling. Some techniques are subtle; some are more a punch in the face; but all of them are designed to separate you from your wallet. If you want to see selling at its best, walk the midway of any carnival or circus. At the circus you can't buy a peanut but you can sure buy "circus peanuts." They cost a little more and we suspect they taste a little better because somehow ordinary legumes have been transformed into "circus peanuts." We say "suspect they taste better" because you don't actually eat circus peanuts. You feed them to the circus elephants. Let's see if I have this right. You want me to purchase peanuts at a premium and then present them to your parade of prodigious pachyderms? That's some psychology!

Working the midway late one night, I was fascinated to watch the carnies working their "joints." A mark would walk by, and in a heartbeat the carnie would find just the right words to stop the mark in his tracks and prompt him to turn to take a chance. "Hey! Mr. Big Hat! I bet you can't knock these bottles over! Not even if I give you three chances instead of the usual two!" And Mr. Big Hat and even bigger ego lays his buck on the rail as another sucker bites the dust.

Some sales techniques are little more than a ruse that is borderline ethical. The really smooth ones involve solid psychology. Read on, and I'll show you a few of the best ideas.

Deep Thoughts

If you are of the right demographic (middle-aged), you read the section title "Deep Thoughts" and were reminded of the old *Saturday Night Live* skit that seemed to imply that writers are deep thinkers or at least think they are! It is closer to the truth that good writers ask good questions and perhaps have the ability to put two or more ideas on a collision course to come up with a new way of looking at the world. So let me tip my hat to truly deep thinkers:

- Paco UnderHill, who wrote *Why We Buy: The Science of Shopping* (Touchstone, 2000), is the expert on store design that sells.
- Robert Cialdini, who wrote *Influence: The Psychology of Persuasion,* knows more than anyone about the fundamentals of decision making.
- Richard Chase and Sriram Dasu, who wrote *Want to Perfect Your Company's Service? Use Behavioral Science* (Harvard Business School Press, 2001), offers a first-rate look at psychology and the service experience.

Each of the above authors has a unique perspective on the scientific explanation of why we do what we do. We borrow a few good ideas from each of these authors in the section that follows.

Eagle Eye

We were young and traveling on a shoestring. I had just spoken to a group at an Atlantic City casino, and Buns and I were squeezing a few moments of goof-off time on the boardwalk, when an eagle caught my eye. Not a real eagle, a porcelain eagle that was flying from a porcelain perch in a gift shop window. The skies were gray and the wind whipped a chill as I pushed my nose against the window for a better look. I love the symbolism of eagles, and it seemed a shame that this last proud specimen might be left to fly solo, unsold and undusted until the soon-to-be-closed shop reopened next season.

"Can you see the price?" Buns asked, as she always wants me to have what I want.

"Yeah, 495 bucks. Can you believe it?"

I unstuck my nose from the shop window, found a warm hand to hold, and turned back toward the casino.

"Sir! Sir!" It was the salesman from the shop chasing after me as though I were about to lose my wallet. "You must have seen something you liked."

"The eagle is a beauty but way out of my league."

"Well, how does 395 sound to you?"

Poof! 100 bucks disappeared off the price!

"Sorry, that's still too steep for me. Maybe someday I'll have that kind of money, but today just isn't the day." I turned away but Buns was squeezing my hand excitedly. It was her "Whatever you want to do is fine with me" squeeze. (I've always had her support even when we didn't always have much else.)

"Sir! Sir!"

I looked back over my shoulder and witnessed another amazing 100-plus dollars vanish as he said, "We're about to close for the season. If you really like the eagle, you can take it home for 175."

"Sorry, too cheap!"

I might have bought that eagle had he not stopped me so soon. I might have gotten a few hundred yards down the beach, giving time for the first discount to wart on me, weaken my resolve, and turn me around. Two-ninety-five was a real, believable deal, but the shopkeeper turned me around and dropped too low, so low that I was now suspicious of the product. The eagle had turned into a turkey.

I hadn't thought of that incident for years until this morning, when I received an e-mail bid for repainting my airplane. An earlier bid was so high that I sucked cold air across my front teeth and called in response to say, "Are you sure this is correct? I just know I can get this done for much, much less!"

So this morning the new bid arrived by e-mail, 3,000 bucks less and a few hundred lower than the next lowest bidder. But he isn't getting my business. Like the eagle, if the first price was right, how could the guy lower it so much? Was he sticking it to me then, or is he trying to stick it to me now?

Retail sales and service are a psychologist's playground. I'm going to show you a few of the psychological tricks of the trade that cause us to buy or not to buy.

SUGGESTION SERVICE

Nobody likes to feel sold, whereas everybody likes to feel served. Few folks feel comfortable with the idea of hard selling a customer. Some warm to the thrill of shaking the customer free of his last buck, but, we can be thankful, they are the minority. In the new economy, this minority is an anachronism, a relic of the "sleezoid" past. Besides, today's customer is so sophisticated that even children are capable of spotting a sales pitch from a mile away. So I say, "Give up the hard sell." Hard selling is short-term thinking. Sure, you may make a sale—once, but you stand a huge chance of losing a long-term customer.

With the ubiquitous availability of the Internet, your biggest concern is not leading with the lowest price. In today's economy the sale belongs to the folks who appear to offer the greatest value. If you don't expect to see a customer again, you can play a little harder. For the rest of us, I suggest four steps to what I call *suggestive serving!*

Suggestive Serving: Putting the Customer Ahead of the Sale

Four simple steps comprise suggestive serving, a strategy that presents selling as the service that it really is. The steps: establish rapport; discover the problem; offer a complete solution; and cement the relationship.

1. Establish rapport. Rather than the tired "May I help you?" lead by saying or doing something to establish true rapport. Let customers know that you recognize them as unique human beings. Something as simple as 'Hey! Nice shirt!' lets the customer know that he is at least a step above the next number in line. When you get better at rapport building, you can say, "Interesting accent. Where do you call home?" Of course, the best of the best remember each customer by name. Nothing beats that, although "Nice to see you! Your usual?" comes pretty close.

2. Discover the problem. Great service and great selling become one when viewed as opportunities to solve a problem for customers. It may not alter content, but it certainly alters context when you are seen as trying to solve a customer's last problem rather than take her last dollar.

Here's a great line for a home center employee: "What's your project today?" In a heartbeat we go from salesclerk to collaborator, and anything we suggest for completing the project looks more like a service, although it results in a sale.

3. Offer a complete solution. Once you have discovered the problem, offering a solution is more than an attempt to sell. It becomes an obligation on the part of the server. I've covered this in greater detail in other books but for now, offering a complete solution is the heart of suggestion service. The cool thing is that so long as you are offering problem-solving products and services, there is absolutely no need to drag out that tired refrain, "Will there be anything else?"

4. Cement the relationship. At the end of the transaction, for goodness' sake do or say something that lets the customer know that just because the sale is complete, the service doesn't stop. Cut out your tongue if it will keep you from saying "next!" Instead, offer your card and suggest that the customer can call if there are questions. Invite the customer to ask for you on the next visit. Do anything to let the customer feel welcome to continue a relationship with real people.

FOUR SIMPLE STEPS

When I offer the four steps to serving, it is with the idea that a customer who is fully served is also fully sold. The sale becomes a foregone conclusion rather than an act of manipulation. From the first hello, the process of discovering how you can help to solve a customer's problem gently unfolds until the moment at the cash register that is happy for both parties.

The Power of a Story

While enjoying lunch with a Canadian client, my interest was aroused when he explained that the french fries were made from a special potato. The Kennebec potato is native to western Canada and available in the fall. It is sweeter and fries up with a crunchier texture. Chomp on a Kennebec fry while you are swilling a cold Molson, and it is doubtful that you would notice anything special. Without the story it's just another great tasting french fry.

But once you know the story, you become a french fry gourmand. What was missing from the recipe was not salt or seasoning; what was missing was the story!

This same client mentioned that his company had switched specs on eggs. There is a spec on an egg? I thought there was large, medium, and small but otherwise an egg is an egg is an egg. Not so! There are all sorts of eggs. It turns out that my client had decided that the hens that lay the eggs for his chain must not be more than 12 weeks old. Younger hens lay eggs with stronger yolk sacks, which in turn make fluffier omelets, have less unintentional breakage, and produce sunny-side up and poached eggs that stand up proudly.

But, again, if there were no story, it's just another egg. Get it?

The Power of Sampling

Buns is right. Restaurants should offer a dessert sampler; you know, several of their finest on one plate. And I'll add that everyone should make it easy to sample product and service.

Another Canadian client with whom I was lunching mentioned that many of his customers never open a menu. They slide into the booth and order "the usual." How many of your customers order the usual? How many of your customers are aware of your full line of products and services? If the answer is less than 100 percent, you have work to do!

The first step is to figure out how to create a demo of your products. I've always worked from the premise that if you have a great product that meets your customer's needs for quality, price, and convenience, a sale will naturally follow—but not until you figure how to get trial.

Figure that out and watch sales zoom. No new customers, just new business!

The Art of the Steal

I'd like you to plant the next two Thinking Points into your brain before you read the next story.

T *h i n k i n g* **P** *o i n t*

The longer a customer lingers, the more likely the customer is to buy.

T *h i n k i n g* **P** *o i n t*

Possession begins when you get the product into customers' hands.

The purpose of a store is to transfer possession. Get them touching and therefore owning! One boring afternoon at the Los Angeles Airport I decided to watch a Moonie as he accosted one weary, wary traveler after another, attempting to shake them down for cash. It was a study in applied psychology.

"Hi! Where're you from?" (Moonies knew the universal disarmament phrase; after all, who can resist such a simple question?)

"Topeka."

"Great town!" said the Moonie, sounding for all the world as though he had been to Topeka, loved it, and perhaps knew folks from the old neighborhood.

Guard down but hands occupied with a carry-on and a briefcase, the mark was helpless as the Moonie reached into the mark's personal space holding a small American flag with the intention of attaching it to the traveler with a straight pin. Who could refuse an American flag from one of the home boys?

"Can you hold this for me?" The Moonie thrust an expensive-looking book into the traveler's hand. This move forced the mark to put down his baggage, which served to thoroughly arrest any chance of forward movement. Now the mark had received a small gift and in his mind's eye a large obligation. At the very least, the traveler was obligated to be friendly. And he couldn't walk away with a book that belonged to a stranger.

The usual next move is an attempt by the traveler to return the book, a move always rebuffed by the Moonie, who would say, "I want you to have this as a gift from me."

"Well, thanks. I'll read it on the plane," followed by an attempt to gather up his belongings.

"In case you don't know, we're working to help mothers and children who are down on their luck. Do you think you could spare a few bucks to help them?"

Now the mark is holding what appears to be an expensive book and is balancing this against his potential contribution, which he has already been told should be a few bucks.

The mark fishes in his wallet, and the most remarkable thing happens. The Moonie steps closer and peers into the wallet as well! As the mark starts to remove a couple of bucks, the disappointed Moonie says in a pitiful voice, "Do you have anything larger? We have lots of women and children who are in desperate need of your help. Can't you do just a little bit better?" And reaching toward the wallet, he points to a 20 and pleads, "How about this one? You know these books are really expensive."

Guess who has taken possession of the book? Never mind that he didn't want it, didn't ask for it, and most likely will never, ever read it!

I give Moonies high marks for style, even though it is manipulation at its sleeziest.

Hang in There, Fred!

My friend Fred Vang e-mailed me a photo of a Toyota he had taken on a factory-sponsored new car introduction. This was no ordinary test drive; a good thing as Fred, a real car guy, is not an ordinary driver. Fred is a car consultant and makes it his business to know what he arranges for clients to buy. I hate to even buy gas without consulting Fred!

Somehow Fred had managed to get this 4Runner hung over a rock (he says on purpose!) so that the vehicle was teetering on its right front and left rear wheels. The other two wheels were so high above the ground that Fred had to jump nearly five feet to exit the vehicle and survey his vehicle's condition.

"Fred! How in the world did you get that thing out of there?" We were on the phone and staring at the e-mailed photo, each in our respective offices.

"I just drove it right out! It has 4 × 4 drive, and the computer knew which of the wheels had traction! Now that's the way to test a vehicle!"

Could you have told Fred about the 4 × 4 drive system? Probably, but showing it off under real and extreme conditions turned Fred from a believer to a proselyte!

Now put all three concepts together into a single sale: Encourage your customers to linger—Help your customers take mental possession—Make trial as realistic as possible.

Watch how this next salesperson used these techniques to win a customer.

Work on Customer Time

Buns had decided that we needed a large rug to cozy up the large carpeted area that is both our living room and impromptu stage for our grandkids' performances. So we stopped at a large carpet store just before closing. We were immediately stymied by a dizzying array of choices, and there was no way we could make our decision before the store closed.

"We'll come back when we have more time to browse," I told the owner.

"Take your time. I usually do paperwork after hours, so look as long as you want." (Encourage customers to linger.)

The employees exited, and the owner locked the door behind them. We had the store to ourselves! We eventually narrowed the choice to two: mine and Buns's. My carpet was gorgeous; Buns's carpet was okay. As we debated who had the superior taste, the store owner said, "Take them both home and try them out. You can bring back the one you don't choose."

"We'd better not. We live 60 or so miles from here, and it's not likely we could be back for a while," I said. "Please. Take both carpets and take your time bringing the other back. We're going to be here and besides, you need the carpet." (Help the customer take possession.)

Placing that carpet required moving half the furniture in the house. First we tried my choice. Gorgeous! Then we moved and removed furniture a second time to roll Buns's selection into place. Gorgeouser!

We bought the carpet.

CONVERTS

Do you know what percentage of your customers convert to buyers? Not every customer leaves with a package under her arm. That's okay because we know that not every customer is psychologically capable of buying on the first contact or impression. A few potential buyers come to our door ready to say yes, whereas others wouldn't feel comfortable signing on the dotted line without making more visits or comparisons. "Just looking" may just as well mean "I want to buy, but I'm not quite comfortable with making the decision."

We also know that not every impression or contact has the same weight. Seeing your ad on a bus bench counts as an impression but doesn't have as much weight as having a friend recommend you personally. A letter from the owner carries some weight but not the same as a long, comfortable visit to your store or office.

Generally, the bigger the ticket or greater the risk associated with the sale, the more impressions it takes to turn prospects into buyers. *Personal contact* counts more than other impressions. In a retail environment one best strategy is to actively intercept the customer. Customers left to wander aimlessly are not as likely to buy as customers who are comfortably intercepted.

Do you know how many contacts it takes to turn a shopper into a buyer? We analyzed our speaking business and were amazed to discover that the average number of contacts potential clients have with our office before finally deciding to invite me to speak is 8.05! That includes phone calls, e-mails, referrals from other clients, and perhaps reading one of our books, but, all told, we're talking 8.05 as the average.

Of course, a few folks see my book in the airport bookstore and have an assistant book us the following day. But those folks are few and far between. When it happens that way, I am thrilled, and suspicious! What does this mean? For me it means that if, after meeting you at a conference, I followed up with an e-mail, a phone call, and maybe a letter, but stopped there with four impressions, I'd lose half my business. And so it is for you. Every potential customer remains a *potential* customer until you have impressed them enough—or at least often!

STEP INSIDE

Once you have a prospect in the door (or on your Web site), here are a few things to know about the physical environment. (You could call this *feng shui* for the retailer!)

- Show off the biggest sign. Your store and its windows are the biggest sign!
- Make it easy to buy. It could be something as simple as good directional signs or store policies that are easy to understand.
- Customers need hands. Make it easy to put things in the shopping cart by having a cart! This applies to Internet sites and even telephone sales.
- Hold that sale. Customers need a psychological resting place before they can begin to buy. This idea comes straight from author Paco Underhill, who says that customers need a "transition zone" and that "whatever is in that zone is lost on them."
- Close to you. Putting items that complement each other close together increases sales. This is called *managing adjacencies* and applies to all kinds of selling. If you are selling paint, you'd better display brushes nearby, even if it means having several displays of brushes. If you are selling services or a mix of products and services, display them close together. For example, if you are selling speaking and you offer a book or other learning tools to complement the presentation, the time to mention the book is when you are selling the speaking engagement. If you have a brochure, why not show the book on the same page where you promote your speaking? This works for two reasons. First, the customer most likely to buy one complementary product is most likely to want and need another. Second, once you have the customer in the buying mood, why separate the two potential sales by either distance or time?
- Create lasting impressions. The last impression makes the strongest impression. Don't finish an experience with anything unpleasant, such as a long wait in line. Time spent waiting to be served seems longer than time spent waiting after contact is initiated.

I was once part of a project to design a state-of-the-art fast-food restaurant. We decided to use drive-through technology in the dining room, so we placed a telephone on each table and gave it a direct line to an operator in the kitchen. A back-lighted menu was also on or near each table so that all a guest had to do was check out the menu and pick up the phone.

By our watch the service was incredibly fast. No more waiting for your server to get to your table with water and a menu; no more waiting for the server to return to take your order. It was incredibly efficient. The customers hated it. They said, "It took too long." Why? Traditional dining room service begins with bringing the guest water and a menu. In the mind of the guest that was the precise moment when service had begun. "They know I am here. I have water (something to do) and a menu. We're really cooking now!"

It didn't matter that in our new system the wait was only two minutes for the water and the menu. Forget that it was only eight minutes for the food to arrive from the kitchen. With the new system it appeared that nothing, absolutely nothing, happened until the food arrived. By then it didn't matter if the food was hot; the customer was!

There is no such thing as a fast long line. All long lines are, by customer definition, slow lines.

A few decades ago a major fast-food restaurant designed and tested a new concept in food service. It placed waiting customers in a single line rather than the multiple-line system used by McDonald's. Customers entered the building and immediately found themselves in a queue, a line that could easily have 20 or more waiting customers at meal times. But the line moved very quickly; at least that's what the stopwatch said. Customers thought otherwise.

At station one, customers placed their order for burgers or other hot sandwiches with an order taker who communicated orders to the kitchen in precomputer days. Station two, the next short stop along the line, was where fries or onion rings were ordered and placed on a customer's tray. At the third station customers were served a drink. Payment and delivery were at the final station.

The total time from the front door to the dining room table was much faster than with the McDonald's-like scatter system. It was faster by every measure except the customers.' They hated it; as far as they were concerned, it took too long.

We can speculate, but we won't ever know for certain. Do you think the outcome might have been different had customers had something to see and do while skimming along the counter? What if the kitchen had been open to view, and customers could see their sandwich being prepared? What if customers had to prepare their own drinks? And what if the order taker at station one had the added responsibility of telling customers, "You are less than 90 seconds from lunch?"

Designing for Comfort

Stinky service is often the result of poor design or, as is more often the case, no design at all. Design elements impact customer service in the most unexpected ways.

Needing a fix for a big, fat, greasy-in-a-good-way patty melt, we stopped at the Burger Barn. In an instant we were greeted with the usual hug delivered in person by the owner, Vickie.

"The new addition is looking great."

"And not a moment too soon. I had to turn away a dozen customers today because there was just no place to seat them. The addition will solve that, but now I'm worried about the kitchen keeping up."

Buns volunteered my services. (She does that.) "Look. You have the makeup table and the prep area reversed. Do you see how they have to cross paths? Swap them around and you should see an instant improvement in efficiency."

In production environments, it's common to think through the relationship between function and design. Why not in the sales environment? Whether you are designing a retail store or a Web site, a sales brochure or an office suite, three things must be accomplished:

1. Merchandising: Present, sample, and compare
2. Customer service: Purchase and problem resolution
3. Customer dynamics: Interaction

MERCHANDISING

Merchandising accomplishes three things: product presentation, sampling, and comparison. Step into one of Sears most recently remodeled hardware departments and behold a thing of great beauty, with Craftsman tools lovingly displayed under sensual lighting that invite you to touch and beckon to be taken home. (So sensual a place is this to die-hard tool lovers that small children should be banned.) Packaging matters and packaging include the entirety of the experience.

When it comes to understanding experience, the best in the world are the designers of theme parks and other gated attractions. Among the best of the best is Bob Rogers of BRC Imagination Arts, who suggests that we think not just about the buying experience but all the way to the experience that the purchased item confers. This may answer the mystery of why a grown person would pay a premium for the privilege of wearing a shirt with someone else's name on it. Think Tommy Hilfiger products.

"Retailers don't get it," says Rogers. "Retail is a collectivist idea. The shopping center is a collection of very different stores, very different experiences." Rogers adds that even when the synergy is good, the experience might be better if it were focused.

Entertainment, on the other hand, is centrist—a very clear central idea with everything a reflection of that central idea. At a Broadway production of a Disney show, you wouldn't expect to see a Victoria's Secret fashion show during intermission. "Retailers," notes Rogers, "don't get the idea. When you visit Disney, all you're going to see at its stores and rides and restaurants . . . is Disney, one theme carried throughout the entire experience."

In retailing we call this *brand congruence.* Starbucks and Nike get it with one theme in their stores. "The corporate and retail brand experiences assume that the corporation is important . . . but the smartest retail and brand experiences celebrate the world of the customer . . . it's not about the corporation . . . it's about the customers and lives," says Rogers.

If any industry is good at sampling, which is merchandising at its best, it has to be the restaurant industry, and two of the best are Olive Garden and Great Harvest Bread Company. One of the things we love best about the Olive Garden is the wait! You can pretty much count on being led by the nose to a sampling of hot, fresh breadsticks. And if you walk into any Great Harvest Bread Store, you'll be met at the bread board with an offer for a free slice of fresh, buttered bread. We're not talking a little scrap dangling from a toothpick. We're talking a thick, sometimes still hot, slice of delicious fresh-baked bread. Customers will buy what you tell them to buy.

When Buns and I owned a fast-food fried chicken franchise, we could sell whatever we put on the outside reader board. When we put corn on the cob on the sign, we sold corn. When we mentioned cole slaw, we sold cole slaw. When we found ourselves with an overabundance of dark meat, we advertised three-legged chickens and sold dark meat like it was going out of style. When we advertised three-legged chickens, limit two, we sold even more!

If you have a product or service that isn't selling as it should, maybe customers haven't been told they are supposed to buy it.

> **T h i n k i n g   P o i n t**
>
> *What products could you sell or upgrade simply by reminding customers through better merchandising?*
>
> **T h i n k i n g   P o i n t**
>
> *How could you improve product presentation, sampling, and comparison where you do business?*

CUSTOMER SERVICE

Customer service is the second attribute of a store, Web site, or other point of purchase. And that leads us to a huge failing in customer service: Too often customers are in a buying mood but no one seems interested in taking their money! Quick, what is the main advantage of shopping at big-box discounters?

Answer: They operate on customer time.

Yesterday Buns and I worked on the property, whittled on the new book, fixed a quiet dinner, and ran out of daylight before we ran out of gas.

"Do you want to go to Wal-Mart?" "Sure, what do we need?" "Let's get that Steam Vac we looked at, and I'll shampoo the carpets when we get home." (This took place at 8 PM—customer time.)

Land's End sells me pants while I watch Jay Leno. Amazon.com sends us books when it's too early or too late or just too anything to go out. Customer time—it's a marvelous idea.

Customer service also includes *problem resolution*. Great servers cover the back end of the sale by making it easy to ask questions, schedule repairs, and, when all else fails, return products. Great servers show concern about the customer after the sale. We'll go out on a limb here and say that no professional retailer or service provider is without a well-constructed Web site because Web sites are there for you 24/7.

Last week the backup GPS unit in our airplane gave us a curious error message. We went straight to Garmin.com, where we failed to resolve the issue on the FAQs page. So we fished out its toll-free number and in a matter of minutes were on the phone with a friendly expert who offered to repair the unit at no charge—all this for a product that is three years out of warranty!

Guess what kind of PDA I'd like to buy? Garmin!

T h i n k i n g **P** o i n t

Have you covered the back end of the sale as well as the front?

Customer Dynamics

Now we come to the third and least understood attribute of service: customer dynamics. The overall goal of customer dynamics is simple—promote conversation. You should know in global terms who buys your products, where they live and work, how they use your products, and why they choose you over the competition. And you should know your customers individually. With modern computer technology, there's no excuse. The two cheapest resources you have for establishing relationships with your customers are computer memory and telephone time. Use them both liberally.

Customers should also know other customers as well as the employees of the enterprise. Personal relationships are the foundation of loyalty. Vendors of computer hardware and software learned early that customers often know more about the product than does the company. When the help desk resources were stretched thin, the obvious solution was to connect customers directly. The result? New ideas and more loyal customers.

Customers often don't have as much of a relationship with a product as they do with the people who use or produce or serve that product. This is what logo products are all about. The FUBU product line that is designed and manufactured by Black entrepreneurs is a perfect example. FUBU is For Us, By Us. And FUBU customers are stating an affinity with others who share their values in the same way that Nike customers are similar but different from Adidas customers.

One factor of product loyalty is loyalty to other customers. (And that explains why a grown man would pay premium prices to wear a shirt, even though his name is not reallyTommy Hilfiger!)

T h i n k i n g **P** o i n t

What more could you do to promote conversation with

your customers and among your customers?

THE "NO EXCUSES" LIST

Now that you have heard the truth, there are no excuses for delivering service that stinks. There is . . .

- *No excuse* not to know your customer personally and professionally.

You must get to know your customers personally and understand what is important to them as human beings, understand and respect their culture and the cultural influences they bring to transactions. And you must know your customers professionally and understand what problems they are trying to solve and the context in which they must solve them.

> **T** *h i n k i n g* **P** *o i n t*
>
> *What should you know about your customers and how could you gather and use that information?*
>
> **T** *h i n k i n g* **P** *o i n t*
>
> *How could you assure your customers that their personal information will be kept private? And what could you do to encourage them to tell you more?*

- *No excuse* for making customers wait.

Learn to work on customer time and have a presence on the Internet 24/7. And when you must make a customer wait, make the wait interesting, informative, and worth it.

> **T** *h i n k i n g* **P** *o i n t*
>
> *How are you making your customers wait and how could you make waiting more of an experience and less of a hassle?*

- *No excuse* to say no to a customer—and no excuse not to charge for saying yes.

Delegate the authority to turn down a customer's request to the highest level, and then never use it! Provide service-level options that are flexible and tailored to the needs of the customer rather than the system.

> **T** h i n k i n g **P** o i n t
>
> *What service-level options could you provide?*

- *No excuse* not to cooperate with your competition.

Make serving customers more important than a sale, and don't be embarrassed to make money doing it!

> **T** h i n k i n g **P** o i n t
>
> *How could you make money cooperating with your competition?*

- *No excuse* not to personalize and customize just in time.

It's no surprise that "I want it my way" is a hot trend in an age of "I want it now." The chains that are nibbling away at Mickey D are those that build burgers according to the customer's plan. But burgers aren't the only product that you can have your way. Hop on the Internet and watch your new automobile being custom built at the factory. And while you are clicking away, you can order blue jeans and fragrances, candy and furniture made just the way you want them delivered to your door.

As reported in the December 23, 2002, issue of *Time,* "In the age of TiVo and iPod, consumers increasingly expect to custom-tailor their lives, and retailers are eager to comply."

> **T** h i n k i n g **P** o i n t
>
> *How could you personalize your customer service*
> *and customize products?*

- *No excuse* not to hire and train customer-focused Service Naturals.

Good people have to work somewhere, so there is no reason why they can't work for you!

T h i n k i n g   P o i n t

Have you identified what a Service Natural might look like in your

business? Are you profiling to ensure that your hiring is on

target? Are you committed to hiring slowly and firing fast?

- *No excuse* to treat all customers equally.

Know who are your most profitable customers. Tailor your service offer based on the numbers, and be prepared to "fire" customers who aren't profitable. Focus on maintaining the loyalty of your best customers. Customers don't want to be treated equally. They want to be treated individually, and even though they love choice, they don't love having to choose. (And that is another reason there is no excuse not to know your customer!)

T h i n k i n g   P o i n t

If you knew who were your most profitable customers,

what would you do differently?

- *No excuse* not to exercise your "MicroBrand."

In the future, brands will become more important but not in the way we see them today in the mass markets. Mass marketing is losing steam. In the future, local brands that we call MicroBrands will matter most. We first noticed the trend while walking down the street in Estes Park, Colorado. It was one of those throwaway days when the highest and best use of an hour is to do absolutely nothing, and that's exactly what we were doing when we noticed the sign. Not the big yellow sign that announced yet another Subway sandwich shop. Nope, we were arrested by the dingy yellow banner that had been draped beneath its plastic cousin,"Now open under old management."

Someone understood that the brand of the old manager was stronger than the brand of the last manager and stronger still than the otherwise powerful and international brand of Subway. It seemed to say, "Come in . . . to see *me!*"

MicroBrands are little brands that sit on top of bigger brands and are often more powerful than the big brands they sit on. And a MicroBrand is any brand intended to dominate a micromarket, which can be as small as a one-on-one relationship. In the near future, marketing will become more targeted; targeted against markets too small to be efficiently won other than through relationships. And relationships are at the heart of customer service.

Th i n k i n g **P**o i n t

What MicroBrands are at work in your organization?

IT'S A WRAP!

We've heard it said a dozen ways: Never try to teach a pig to sing; it wastes your time and irritates the pig. Never wrestle with a pig; you get dirty and the pig loves it. Or you can't get a silk purse from a sow's ear. However colorfully you describe it, the simple truth remains: Great customer service comes from only one place, the heart of a Service Natural.

No matter how hard you train or how tightly you control, there are some folks, most folks, who are totally unable to deliver that thing we call Positively Outrageous Service. Stop wasting your time . . . and irritating the pigs.

Only Service Naturals will deliver world-class customer service.

And now you know Why Service Stinks . . . and Exactly What to Do about It!

It was another hot, muggy day in Texas. Dew points were high, and a low pressure system was pumping gulf moisture into the region. It was no surprise that thunderstorms with high winds, damaging hail, and a potential for tornadoes marred the forecast and made flying too far from the hangar not the best of ideas. We had committed to making an Angel Flight, the first leg of a two-leg relay ferrying a patient and companion from Midland through Kerrville and then on to Houston. No sooner had we made the hand-off to a pilot-volunteer from Austin when our pants' phone went off. (You can call our office phone most of the time, but when I'm not in the office I'm still in my pants. At least, if I am accepting calls!)

"Scott, I hate to ask you, but we just got a call from a neighbor whose father has gone into cardiac distress. She needs to get to Midland, and there's nothing this late in the day to get her there. Is there any chance you could fly her and her daughter to Midland?"

The plane was still on the ramp, fueled and ready. I had the charts in my hand. How could I say no? So I fired up the big Continental engine and dodged our way west, avoiding huge cells full of rain and lightning. Several hours later, I was back on my home ramp, having run the gauntlet in two directions. My thirst led me to the pilots lounge, where I knew there would be a huge vat of iced tea, condensation dripping from the sides and a promise of instant relief.

Unlike the story in the beginning of the book, the young woman behind the desk wasn't reading a novel. This one came to the door to greet us, reminding us there would be a fuel discount for our Angel Flight and even suggested that we top off the hot afternoon with a cold glass of iced tea.

"Mr. Gross?"

"Yes, ma'am?"

"I hear you write books. What are they about?"

"Well, I have one management adventure book titled *Borrowed Dreams,* but the rest of them are about managing the customer service experience."

"I'd like to read them sometime. I like learning new things. But to tell you the truth, when it comes to customer service" (there was a brief pause, just long enough for a smile to spread across her already pleasant face), "to tell you the truth, I'm just naturally nice!"

Naturally nice.

That pretty much covers it!

Buns's Barbeque Ribs

(Baste mix for 4 lbs. of fat-trimmed pork ribs)

6 T soft margarine (or microwave until melted)   4 T dry mustard
4 t salt   4 t sugar
1½ t paprika   ½ t pepper
4 T Worcestershire sauce

Mix until well blended. Brush all but ½ cup all over ribs, primarily on meatier side. Place in covered roaster and bake in 275 degree oven for 3 hours.

Remove from pan; discard drippings. Add remaining baste mix as you grill until ribs are browned.

(This serves 4–6 people. Scott likes them with just the baste mix; I prefer a spicy barbecue sauce on mine.)

Hint: For added flavor, grill over mesquite chips that have been soaked in water for 24 hours. (This is in addition to the usual charcoal briquets.)

ABOUT THE AUTHOR

There is nothing complicated about T. Scott Gross. He makes a living doing interesting things and sharing the experiences, being a master at making complex ideas seem simple and fun. *Why Service Stinks* is Scott's ninth business book. T. Scott Gross is the creator of the management classic *Positively Outrageous Service,* and now he's back with more stories, more great ideas. Scott's here to tell us *Why Service Stinks . . . and Exactly What to Do about It!*

When he is not on the road speaking at a conference or convention, you can find him being a kid on his John Deere tractor or sneaking away to fly his plane or just hanging out with his grandkids. Scott is an instrument-rated pilot, a volunteer EMT in his home town of Center Point, Texas, and a pretty good cook. He has worked some of the world's most interesting (and sometimes dangerous) jobs. From wildland firefighter to street medic, from deckhand on an oil tanker to a carnie working the midway, Scott has turned his life's work into a living laboratory for ideas and stories.

His best friend on the planet is his wife, Buns. She calls him Tiger. Kiddo and Jo Bob call him Dad. And Big Guy and Princess call him Pops. Whatever you call him, don't catch his attention unless you are ready to hear a story! It's what comes naturally to him!

Share the message!

Bulk discounts
Discounts start at only 10 copies. Save up to 55% off retail price.

Custom publishing
Private label a cover with your organization's name and logo. Or, tailor information to your needs with a custom pamphlet that highlights specific chapters.

Ancillaries
Workshop outlines, videos, and other products are available on select titles.

Dynamic speakers
Engaging authors are available to share their expertise and insight at your event.

Call Dearborn Trade Special Sales at 1-800-245-BOOK (2665) or e-mail trade@dearborn.com